COMMON SENSE ABOUT RUSSIA

COMMON SENSE ABOUT
RUSSIA

by
ROBERT CONQUEST

NEW YORK
THE MACMILLAN COMPANY
1960

© Robert Conquest 1960

All rights reserved—no part of this book may be re-
produced in any form without permission in writing
from the publisher, except by a reviewer who wishes
to quote brief passages in connection with a review
written for inclusion in magazine or newspaper.

First Printing

Printed in the United States of America

Library of Congress catalog card number: 60-15043

FOR
ANTHONY HARTLEY

CONTENTS

CONTENTS

COMMON SENSE ABOUT RUSSIA

INTRODUCTION

WE HAVE TO LIVE with Russia, the Russian state and the Russian people. In deciding on our attitudes and policies we need clear heads and cool heads. We need to avoid extreme gullibility and extreme suspiciousness alike. We need sympathy and understanding as much as we need refusal to accept illusion.

Our views on many urgent public issues depend for their validity on a reasonable and realistic idea of the facts of Soviet life and policy. Yet even now, far too often, we entertain stereotypes—favourable or hostile, vague or "informed". For one reader Russia is simply a Police State. For another it is a Progressive Society. It is seldom that those who have such clear-cut views are willing to listen to facts which spoil their abstractions.

There are three different sorts of attitude which common sense should make us avoid:

Preconceptions about Russia due to learning a theory first and then approaching things Soviet with the idea of fitting them into it;

Unreal conceptions based on the fact that we all learn of Soviet matters piecemeal, and even if we do not get our first impressions from consciously partisan accounts to the neglect of others, we may still get inaccurate notions simply by accident, through the chance of what set of events happen to compose the first sketch in our mind;

Preconceptions arising from unconscious assumptions about what things are likely to be like, based on our own experience in quite different countries.

The common sense so necessary in getting a realistic view of the Soviet Union is thus quite an effort. It is an effort within the power of all men of good will. It is not about Russia only that the division into desirable and undesirable approaches is that between common sense and lack of it, rather than between high and ordinary I.Qs. "Intellectuals" have always been inclined to fall into the trap of fitting square facts into round theories. Minds of the highest intelligence often produce absurdities beyond the power of the ordinary mind, just as a magnificent computer will produce the wrong answer if it starts out with the wrong assumptions.

To assume that the Soviet Union approximates either Utopia or Devil's Island is plainly wrong. But this does not mean that one can assume that it is much the same as any other country either. The Soviet leaders may be neither devils nor angels, but it does not follow that they are much the same as political leaders anywhere. Russia is neither Heaven nor Hell, nor England nor India, nor Egypt nor Japan. It is Russia. What it is like, and what its political organizations and personalities are like, can be judged only by going for real evidence.

In looking into Soviet politics, the Soviet economic system, the ideas of the Soviet leaders and so on, it seems more important to aim at the essential than at the encyclopaedic. In some spheres the briefest analysis, illustrated only by a few illuminating examples, seems required, and in others an assembly of detailed evidence. But the criterion of this book has nowhere been completeness as such. It has been perspective.

And since everything cannot be covered in a work this size (or indeed in a book of any portable size, except in fairly superficial fashion) it seems best to concentrate on truly critical and illuminating issues. This book does not, in principle, deal with either the undoubted achievements or the undoubted horrors of the Soviet régime. Both the fact that standards of health and education have greatly improved in the USSR in the last forty years, and that large numbers of people have perished in miserable conditions as a result of offending the State, are widely known and may be taken for granted.

Nowadays we cannot expect to be up-to-date for long about political, or even economic, developments, and it seems less important to base our account on the latest action or plan than to show in the first place the more or less permanent things about Soviet society and secondly the directions in which the Party would wish to change it and in which it itself shows a natural tendency to change.

To get the savour of life in the Soviet Union is not an easy thing. It is true that there are several extremely useful first-hand accounts—such as Sally Belfrage's *A Room in Moscow* (André Deutsch Ltd., 1958)—which might be quoted. But how much of the true feeling of life in this country, or even in London, could be obtained in this way? Every one of the thousands of articles and books about life in London, by foreigners who have often lived here a considerable time, and even by Englishmen, would probably be thought of as most misleading by many Londoners. For, on the whole, first-hand accounts are likely to be defective in various ways. This is partly because of the circles in which almost all foreigners—journalists, tourists, delegates and so on—are bound to move. There is nothing particularly Soviet about this problem. An American journalist, if unable to obtain the actual figures, might write that every flat in England has a refrigerator, because every flat he is likely to go to does have one. But he would be wrong.

This is not to deny the value of good first-hand reports by foreigners: the more of them the better. But the natural human failing of making big generalizations from few experiences should be subjected to rigorous checks.

Otherwise you get such things as the assertion by the correspondent of a leading English daily that tips are not accepted by Muscovites: which can be compared with an article in the youth paper *Komsomolskaya Pravda* giving the adventures of a character who tries not to tip and is bullied and denounced by waiters, taxi-drivers, Turkish bath attendants, shop girls and in fact all the remotely tippable people he comes in contact with. The deduction must be that the Englishman's experiences—though genuine—were not typical, though he describes them as such.

And these are on matters of fact, not of opinion. When it comes to imponderables like the enthusiasm of a country's populace for its government, or their view of foreign policy, it is clear that such observations, though not entirely valueless, cannot possibly be relied on one way or the other. We must go deeper.

The Soviet scene, when generalized into social and political categories—favourable or otherwise—appears neat and tidy. But behind this (as can be shown from the more factual and less theoretical official sources themselves) there exists a tangled and lively unofficial life, and an inchoate flux of unorthodox thought. This too must be understood, for a full idea of realities.

This book is not, except perhaps on one or two minor issues, a controversial one. But the subject is one on which so much confusion exists between the notional and the actual, that facts themselves may seem disturbingly partisan to readers who have unwittingly absorbed elements of myth. This cannot be helped, except by the readers' own efforts.

To try to view things without preconception as to the facts is not the same as to have no standards of judgement. Few of us would deny, and Marxists are commendably quick to point out, that we all nourish biases about what is desirable and what is not, which can be attributed in part at least to our backgrounds. It seems right for the author to declare his prejudices. Brought out into the open, they may then be discounted by anyone who disagrees with them, and their effect on this book allowed for.

The main opinions I hold which affect the matter in hand are that, like the Communist heroine and martyr, Rosa Luxemburg, I believe that "Freedom only for the supporters of the Government, only for the members of one party— however numerous they may be—is no freedom at all. Freedom is always and exclusively freedom for the one who thinks differently. Not because of any fanatical concept of 'justice' but because all that is instructive, wholesome and purifying in political freedom depends on this essential characteristic, and its effectiveness vanishes when 'freedom' becomes a special privilege. . . .

"Without general elections, without unrestricted freedom of press and assembly, without a free struggle of opinion, life dies out in every public institution, becomes a mere semblance of life, in which only the bureaucracy remains as the active element. Public life gradually falls asleep, a few dozen party leaders of inexhaustible energy and boundless experience direct and rule. Among them, in reality only a dozen outstanding heads do the leading, and an élite of the working class is invited from time to time to meetings where they are to applaud the speeches of the leaders. . . . Yes, we can go even further: such conditions must inevitably cause a brutalization of public life: attempted assassinations, shooting of hostages, etc." (Rosa Luxemburg: *The Russian Revolution*).

Secondly, with Karl Marx, I hold that "The censored press, a bad press, remains bad, even when giving good products. A free press remains good, even when giving bad products. A eunuch which will always be an incomplete man, even if he has got a good voice. Nature remains good, even when giving birth to monsters. The characteristic of the censored press is that it is a flabby caricature without liberty, a civilized monster, a horror even though sprinkled with rose-water. The government hears only its own voice; it knows that it hears only its own voice and thus establishes itself in the illusion of hearing the voice of the nation, and demands from the people that they share the same illusion. . . ." And again ". . . Boasting every day of everything created through the will of the government, this press is constantly lying, since one day necessarily contradicts the other. And it reaches the point of not even being aware of its lies and losing all shame" (Marx: *Collected Works*, Vol. I).

In principle there seems no reason why these liberties should be incompatible with any particular social or economic structure. Indeed, we may go further and say that any régime which ignores them is basically faulty and unstable— as Marx rather implies. With all that can be said in favour of the Soviet system as it is at present, it can hardly be urged that political democracy and freedom of thought (in *this* sense and not defined in some different way) yet flourish in Russia. But, without seeking a perfection which heaven knows does not exist in the West, we may find reason to hope for a Soviet evolution in the right direction.

CHAPTER I

SOVIET EVIDENCE

W E SHOULD FIRST consider the nature of Soviet evidence. This is not with the purpose of starting off on subject-matter that sometimes shows the Soviet authorities in an unfortunate light. But until we have established the reliability and comprehensiveness of official statements, we cannot deal with them sensibly when we come to matters of substance. And it is in the main on official evidence that we shall be relying.

Any writing on Soviet matters becomes in a sense controversial if it does not simply accept all Soviet evidence at its face value. It is then accused by Communist spokesmen of not being objective, and often of uttering "slanders". This is a handicap which we must accept. But we may consider what it is about Soviet evidence that leads us to subject it to certain suspicions before taking it as truth. And this consideration will also show us something about Soviet attitudes in general.

It is not that there is a shortage of information from the USSR. On the contrary, an enormous amount exists. Yet if this is not treated critically, it is perfectly possible to produce a highly documented work which is practically valueless.

One of the men who had been Stalin's strongest supporters in the struggle against the oppositionists was Sergo Ordzhonikidze. He died in February, 1937. At the time the Soviet press put out a death certificate signed by four doctors, including the Minister of Health and the head of the Kremlin Medical Administration. This described various illnesses from which he had suffered and said that he had been feeling better on the day of his death, but had had a heart attack and died within half an hour. In the *Soviet Encyclopaedia* "O" volume, which came out in 1955, the heart attack still figures. This version remained official until 1956.

An article on Ordzhonikidze in the earlier edition of the *Encyclopaedia* says that "The Trotskyite-Bukharinite degenerates of Fascism wanted to kill Ordzhonikidze", and adds that they did not succeed, but that their "monstrous treachery . . . greatly hastened the death of Ordzhonikidze".

The doctors who had signed the death certificate disappeared in the purges—one of them being shot after a public trial for allegedly poisoning another member of the Politburo (Kuibyshev), and others.

Rumours that Ordzhonikidze had really died in different circumstances were common in Russia for many years, particularly as he perished just before the critical meeting of the Central Committee at which Stalin broke the opposition of those of his own supporters who wished to stop the purge.

In his Secret Speech in 1956 Khrushchev suddenly revealed that Ordzhonikidze had actually been forced to shoot himself.

This sort of thing cannot but cast certain doubts on Soviet evidence in general—and even on such reputable documents as death certificates.

At the Plenary Meeting of the Central Committee of December, 1958, Khrushchev accused Malenkov of "deceiving the Party and the people" when he had said at the 19th Party Congress in 1952 that the grain harvest that year had reached 8 billion poods, while it was actually only 5·6 billion.

In the first place, Malenkov was not issuing a private lie.

The statement was made in the Report of the Central Committee, which he delivered. He was speaking for the Party leadership taken collectively and all of them must have been equally aware of the facts. It is perfectly true that, as Khrushchev says, the method of estimating the grain crop was a fallacious one. It was reported in terms of what was called the "biological yield". This was not the crop as actually harvested, but an estimate of it as it stood in the fields. The mere use of such a method over a period of years shows something odd about Soviet statistics. But in any case it was Malenkov who was the first to denounce it in his report to the Supreme Soviet of August 8, 1953.

That the biological yield method of estimate must be a false one was plainly evident to Stalin, and to Khrushchev and to any others taking a direct interest in the matter. That it was a deliberate falsification seems undoubted, and presumably Khrushchev is right in thinking that those it was designed to deceive, or at least confuse, were "the people".

A further thought arises: the false figure was never corrected and the true figure (if it is the true figure) never given for six years. It is difficult to avoid concluding that it would never have been given at all if Khrushchev himself had happened to have been nominated as rapporteur at the 19th Congress. We are, in fact, only to obtain corrections when original falsehoods can be blamed on someone now out of favour.

Yet the peculiarities of Soviet evidence are not limited to doubtful statement and absence of statement. It is equally extraordinary that awkward truths are sometimes published in a dramatic fashion, as when the figures for the Soviet population, which had not been given for many years, were suddenly announced early in 1958, particularly as they turned out to be 8 or 10 million below the *lowest* estimates that had been made in the West, and some 20 million below those usually expected—202 million in all.

Another Soviet curiosity is the treatment of what Orwell called "unpersons". For many years certain prominent Communist leaders who had perished in the purges were simply not referred to at all in any circumstances. After the rehabilitations made in 1955 and 1956 the existence of a number of these was again recognised—in the *Large Soviet Encyclopaedia*, for instance.

These men whose reputations are now restored are a particular group. They consist of the leaders who supported Stalin's policies, but who nevertheless were executed. The years of their deaths are given, and it is a curious fact that of the six Politburo members involved, men of the highest possible rank, these dates had either been unknown or been wrongly deduced in the West, so deep was the obscurity which had surrounded their fate. A little light has been thus let in. But there still remain a number of former Communist leaders who are treated in the old fashion. The *Encyclopaedia* has no articles on Lenin's associates who later became leaders of the Communist opposition to Stalin. There is nothing on Bukharin or Zinoviev or Kamenev or Rykov. And in the case of Beria, who was executed after a volume with a long article on him had come out, subscribers to the *Encyclopaedia* were issued with alternative pages, and instructed to remove the original with a razor and paste the new ones in. These contained articles and photographs of hitherto neglected persons and phenomena beginning with *Ber*. Later a similar operation was ordered for an article on Chinese Politburo member Kao Kang, who had fallen foul of the authorities in Peking and committed suicide.

It is a curious fact that this type of treatment is given only to Communist deviationists. Hostile figures like the

Tsarist General Wrangel or the Menshevik leader Abramovich are given the space their historical importance warrants.

In the new *Small Soviet Encyclopaedia*, of which at the time of writing three volumes have come out, Bulganin is omitted entirely, while lesser figures are given. The presumption is that when the work is complete it will also omit Molotov and Malenkov. Since Rykov is already on the black list, this will mean that four out of the five Prime Ministers of the Soviet Union who held office between Lenin and Khrushchev will not have their careers covered by what, after all, purports to be a comprehensive work of reference. (Leaving, in fact, only Stalin.)

This treatment has been applied not merely to individuals. When the deportations of seven minority nations of the Caucasus, Crimea and Volga took place in 1941 and 1943-4, the nations concerned were completely eliminated from Soviet reference works. In the case of the Kalmyks, for example, no public statement was ever made about their removal (as it was in some of the other cases). They were simply not mentioned at all for more than 13 years, until a decree restoring them was passed in early 1957. A new Astrakhan Province appeared on maps in the area formerly occupied by the Kalmyk Autonomous Soviet Socialist Republic. Works like the *Encyclopaedia*, whose first edition had contained articles on the nation, now simply dropped them. Even the *Encyclopaedia* article on the Astrakhan Province, whose historical section might have been expected to refer to the people who had lived in the area so long, passed them by in silence.

There are some odd examples of mere absence of information. For instance, the very name of the Minister of State Security in the period 1951(?)—1953 was not known until his removal in April, 1953. In fact, it is still not at all clear quite when his predecessor Abakumov was removed and Ignatiev took over, charged with supervising the "Doctors' Plot" purge.

And then there are matters on which no coherent story exists at all: for example, the trial and execution of the right-wing Communists headed by Bukharin and the former Prime Minister Rykov in 1938. At this trial, which greatly engaged world opinion, the accused were charged with conspiracy, treason and assassination. The evidence consisted solely of confessions.

The practise of resting cases on confessions has lately been condemned. Two figures named as fellow-conspirators in the Bukharin case, though tried separately, have been rehabilitated—Marshal Tukhachevsky and the Politburo member Rudzutak. One of those actually figuring in the trial and shot at the time—Ikramov—has also been rehabilitated. One would imagine from this that the case would fall to the ground. Yet there has been no rehabilitation of the main accused. This is rather as if Hare were rehabilitated and nothing at all said about Burke. The official description of this and the previous comparable trials, as given in a new *History of the USSR* for the use of Higher Educational Establishments (1958) runs: "In 1936, 1937 and at the beginning of 1938 there were the trials of the participants of the underground Trotskyite-Zinovievite and Bukharinist groups. The facts showed that these people were engaged in direct anti-Soviet activities."

In the Soviet *Encyclopaedias* Bukharin and the others still figure as enemies of the people. But there has been no enquiry made or statement put out to establish what they *were* guilty of, if they were not guilty of many of the things alleged against them. The rehabilitations of their accomplices took place in 1955-6, so time has not been wanting. Nor does it seem that the present leaders now believe in the guilt of Bukharin and Co.—if indeed they ever did. Mikoyan told the American journalist Louis Fischer that Bukharin was not guilty. In fact, here is a major event of recent history on which *no* coherent official story, plausible or otherwise, exists.

Another phenomenon in the Soviet official avoidance of "bougeois objectivity" is the way in which a given event or set of events may be ignored entirely, and then provided with explanations which are altered or added to from year to year. For example, in 1949-50 many leading Party officials, including Politburo member Voznesensky, were removed from their posts, "tried" and shot. Nothing was said about this at the time. In December, 1952, an article by Suslov appeared in *Pravda* attacking Voznesensky's economic views as "anti-Marxist". In December, 1954, Abakumov, who had been Minister of State Security in 1949-50, was tried with a number of his subordinates and shot for having faked the evidence in what was now called the "Leningrad Case". Voznesensky and his friends were rehabilitated. And Beria was blamed, Abakumov being said to have acted on his instructions (though at Beria's own trial the previous year nothing had been said about this case). This was the first story. Then, in February, 1956, Khrushchev in his Secret Speech blamed Stalin for having ordered the purge. This second story was equally plausible, but notably different. Then, in July, 1957, Khrushchev stated publicly that Malenkov was to blame too—a third story.

It is natural to conclude that the explanations and the placing of blame in particular circumstances may be incomplete or inaccurate and in any case subject to amendment. In each of these phases the story before the Soviet public reflected the momentary political balance in the struggle for power. It seems unlikely that we shall hear the full story of what happened to Khrushchev's own predecessor as Party

23

Secretary in the Ukraine, Kossior, while Khrushchev himself remains at the head of affairs.

In his Secret Speech, Khrushchev stated that during all the years of the Patriotic War not a single Central Committee plenum took place. But according to the official collection, *The Communist Party of the Soviet Union in Resolutions, etc.*, a plenum took place on January 27, 1944. This sort of thing casts a doubt on every single official document. Moreover, if this is the sort of treatment accorded to straightforward facts, we can imagine what manipulations may be resorted to with statistics and other data much more liable to misrepresentation at the best of times. In many Soviet matters we may repeat what Khrushchev himself says of the material on the Doctors' Plot made available to Presidium members by Stalin—"The case was so presented that no one could verify the facts".

Sidney and Beatrice Webb, in their book, *Soviet Communism: A New Civilization*, described Stalin's Russia, at the time of terror now known officially as "the period of mass repression", as an economic and political democracy. Their error was a simple one: they described not realities, but documents.

But we can now see that the position with Soviet evidence is unsatisfactory. We can exempt ourselves with a very good conscience indeed from taking it at its face value on all occasions. We may, and must, use it, but we can use it discriminatingly.

To refuse to use it at all would be as lamentable as to use it without discrimination. Automatically to regard any Soviet official statement as more or less of a lie is to poison the whole international atmosphere. We must be occasionally critical, but not prejudiced. Some official statements in our own country, after all, appear calculated to produce an erroneous impression. The difference, of course, is that the existence of our opposition press, and of question-time in Parliament, at any rate give the possibility of exposing British official inaccuracies, whereas no such possibilities exist in the Soviet Union, for the time being at any rate.

CHAPTER II

THE CONTEXT OF THE PAST

RUSSIA IS IN THE main a land of great plains and low hills, of steppe and forest, intersected by the sweep of gigantic rivers and their affluents. Only to the south of this central portion of the Soviet Union, beyond the salt marshes of the Putrid Sea, the semi-desert Kalmyk Steppe and the wastes of the Kara Kum, lie quite different types of territory—the hilly peninsula of the Crimea, the mountainous bulk of the Caucasus, the irrigated cotton lands of Turkestan, areas of Asian population conquered by the Tsars in the eighteenth and nineteenth centuries.

In the steppes and forests of the central region, Scandinavian adventurers, many centuries ago, set up a state organization among the Slavonic tribes. Their main centre, Kiev, came under the cultural influence of Byzantium, that Miklegard where the "English", having passed down the Russian rivers, carried their axes in the Varangian guard.

The Scandinavians became Slavonized. Byzantine influence increased. And finally the Grand Prince Vladimir of Kiev, "Equal of the Apostles", was converted to Orthodox Christianity.

Warrior nations from Asia swept through the territory now called the Ukraine, the original hearth of Russian culture. Finally, in the thirteenth century, the Mongol armies overwhelmed the new centres of power, which had shifted northwards to Moscow and elsewhere. The Russian princes became vassals to the Khans. The Mongols demanded tribute and made no attempt to rule directly. The

26

circumstances pressing on the princes—the necessity of placating and duping a ruthless overlord, of outwitting territorial rivals, and of managing their own suspicious subjects—produced rulers of tense strength and ruthless cunning.

Rule over cities and villages from the tented encampments of the nomads was an anomaly which could not last. In the fifteenth century Moscow defeated the Horde, and set up as an independent Russian state. At the same period Byzantium fell to the Turks. The last princess of the Eastern Empire came to Moscow and married its ruler. The monarchs of Russia took the title Tsar. The tradition of the Orthodox Emperor, inheriting in the Third, and last, Rome the semi-divine status of his predecessors on the Bosphorus, began to exercise its power.

In the next century the Tatar Khanates of Kazan and Astrakhan, which blocked expansion east and south, were destroyed, and the state was consolidated by Ivan the Terrible and his secret police. Ivan had always stood as an unpleasant figure in Russian history until Stalin rehabilitated him, excusing his maniac ruthlessness on the ground of his services to the Russian state. Stalin does not seem to have ruminated on the fact that within a few years of Ivan's death Russia was again in a condition of disintegration, as the result of a continual struggle for power.

A new dynasty, the Romanoffs, finally pulled the state together. The next century was marked by stagnation, the increasing degradation of the free peasantry, and the escape of the livelier elements of the population to join the bands of Cossacks whose virtually independent commonwealths beyond the Tsar's frontiers were taking Russian settlement back into the Ukraine, and, for the first time, into the Asian territories of the present-day USSR.

At the end of the century came the reign of Peter the Great, as much the hero of Lenin's Russia as Ivan the

Terrible was of Stalin's. His attention turned west. He broke through to the Baltic and built St. Petersburg, the "window on Europe". He took up Western ideas and enforced them by non-Western methods. His new city, designed to trade with England and Holland, to foster the liberal and mechanic arts, was built by forced labour at enormous cost of life. The blend persisted. Catharine the Great corresponded with the subtlest minds of her age, in between ordering the knouting of court ladies. The peasants lost their remaining rights and an educated class sprang up.

Among noblemen whose lives were at the mercy of the crown, among the great administrative caste which over-lapped them and which was needed to rule the vast territory almost totally lacking in true local authorities, among the regimented and uniformed student class which served as a reservoir for these, unorthodox thoughts began to flourish. The unrest of the seventeenth and eighteenth centuries had shown itself in peasant rebellion and palace coup. After the Napoleonic wars, in which Russians of all opinions had rallied to defeat the invader, a new thing happened. The Decembrist Conspiracy of 1825 sought a true political change—a Constitution.

In the reaction that followed the failure of this aristocratic and intellectual plot, the rulers reverted to the apparent hypocrisy of combining humane formula with brutal action. Nicholas I congratulated himself that capital punishment had been abolished in Russia, while ordering punishments formally non-capital, but actually certain to kill in a cruel fashion. A similarly apparent hyprocrisy has disfigured a great deal of the history of other nations: nevertheless, we may perhaps find, in this respect, a rather peculiarly close parallel between Nicholas and Stalin.

It was at this period, however, that something which greatly differentiates Russia from many, though not all, other countries came to full development. At the same time as there grew up an ever larger administrative apparatus, with a police force of great size and power, a censorship and (eventually) an internal passport system, the intellectuals became wholly alienated from the state. No action of any sort remained open to them within the political community. The state became desiccated from excess of orthodoxy, from want of thought. But at the same time the intellectuals lost direct contact with the day-to-day problems of policy. Their roots withered. They became interested in long-term theories first and reality only as a field for their application. The moods of opposition to Tsarism among the ordinary people had none to turn to for expression and leadership but these men of goodwill and insufficient experience. In the country of the illiterate, the intellectual is king, or will be.

This is naturally to exaggerate both the clearcutness and the extent of the split. Yet a look at the political controversies of the 1917 revolution is a quite extraordinary experience for the unprepared citizen of a fairly mature democracy. Discussions of immediate problems are often of an intricate and intelligent nature. But they are conducted almost entirely in terms of formulae, with, often, a minimum of common-sense.

Between the frozen minds of the Tsarist bureaucrats and the simple absolutes of the political theorists of revolution, a third and greater current of thought and feeling emerged, in the giant literature of Russia. Here may be found, if anywhere, the distinctive "Russian soul" of which so much has been written, in that search for absolute frankness and absolute charity about the human being. And it is certain from hundreds of accounts right up to the present day that this human sensitivity is not confined to the writers, but is manifest, even if sometimes diluted and sometimes perverted, widespread among the Russian people. This is a Russia every bit as real, every bit as much to be taken into account in our general thinking, as the true political Russia of Stalin and Khrushchev. And this sensitivity is to be found even among many articulate intellectuals who have thought of themselves as accepting the opposite views of Stalinism. One of the few writers prominent in the recent "rotten liberal" upsurge to produce a printable recantation was the Communist poetess Margarita Aliger. Yet even there she made the illuminating confession: "I am sometimes inclined to substitute moral-aesthetic considerations for political ones." This is to state, as the Kremlin denies, that these are autonomous spheres which may sometimes conflict.

In the long run it is perhaps this feeling which constitutes the complete, though usually unexplicit, alternative to total ideology. In the anarchist Tolstoy, the liberal Turgenev and the religious Dostoievsky, with all their differences, there is this in common, and it is the taproot of all Russian movements towards truth and justice; and they have been passionate movements.

The same concerns are found in Pasternak, of whom there is little to be said in this book, if only because he demonstrates them, as it were, outside time. He indicates the full power of these sentiments. And his underground popularity in Russia shows that he has struck a note which continues to find response. But he does not enter directly into the struggle by which the old feelings have once again come into action on the social, and almost the political, planes.

On the political wing, among the intellectual groups fighting desperate and often heroic struggles against autocracy, was one which had concerned itself not merely with ideas about the correct structure of society, but also with questions of party discipline and the techniques of seizing power. Their leader, Lenin, a man of enormous will-power and intelligence, led them to victory over all comers in the chaos of defeat in war and the birthpangs of "bourgeois democracy".

In his *State and Revolution*, written as late as 1916, Lenin lays down the development of the Socialist State in classic Marxist terms. After the Revolution things will immediately become more democratic. The State will begin to "wither away". The organs of compulsion will become less obtrusive and gradually be replaced by co-operation. The administration will be done by working men, paid at ordinary workmen's wages, who will go back to industry after a brief period of rule.

It was a great vision: but nothing of the sort happened. On the contrary, in his last years Lenin was himself beginning to say that the Revolution had resulted only in giving a Bolshevik tinge to the old system of bureaucracy and police rule.

The Bolshevik seizure of power in October, 1917, was certainly contrary to the wishes of the majority of the population. In the elections to the Constituent Assembly which took place shortly after, they had only about a quarter of the votes. When the Assembly met it was dissolved by Bolshevik troops.

But there was more to it than this. Even in Lenin's own Marxist view the Revolution was, in principle, premature. Marx had foreseen proletarian revolutions taking place in the advanced industrial countries, where the working class formed a large majority of the population and economic development had reached a stage where all that the revolution needed to do was to take it over as a going concern. Lenin himself had originally foreseen an anti-Tsarist revolution producing a capitalist type of State of the sort prevalent in Western Europe, within which the Marxist party would work to bring about a Socialist revolution after a long interim period. When he seized power in 1917, it was with the expectation that the countries of Western Europe would also have Socialist revolutions within years or months. In that case his revolution, considered simply as a constituent part of a world revolution, would have been reasonable according to Marxist thought.

When the European revolutions did not occur, Lenin and his Government were left out on a limb. From a dogmatic and purist point of view, the correct procedure would have been either to use all Russia's resources in an all-out attempt to produce the aborted European revolution, or else to allow a capitalist restoration in Russia. Trotsky rather favoured the first of these possibilities. But in practice neither was likely to appeal to men, whether in Russia or anywhere else, who had had their first taste of power. And it was possible to take the view that the normal inhumanities of industrialization as produced under capitalism could be avoided if that stage were gone through under representatives of the proletariat. Even so, the situation was odd. A party dedicated to the view that State organisation reflects the economic order found itself planning to create, after the event, the economic structure required to justify it. Lenin had expected his State to be the most democratic of all State forms—this must always be remembered, especially by those who cannot understand why many people of liberal mind everywhere supported the Russian Revolution, and many people of reactionary mind opposed it. But in fact it was, right from the start, set against the majority of the population, and kept itself going in the hope of creating the proletariat which would surely support it.

Two main results followed. First, the evolution of a ruling group with the habit of suppression; and, second, the practice of decisions emerging not from the actual structure of society, but from ideas in people's heads about what that structure should be. All the elements were already present of dictatorship moulding society in accordance with preconceptions.

There were divergencies among Lenin's successors about

how the lines of communication between the rulers and the masses should be re-established. The bulk of the old Bolsheviks followed the "Rightists" headed by Bukharin. They wished to go slowly, to make genuine concessions to the peasantry, and gradually to persuade them to adopt socialist or co-operative forms of agriculture while at the same time building up industry at a pace not too hard for the Russian economy. And something like this took place under the New Economic Policy put into force by Lenin. By 1929 considerable progress had already been made.

But Stalin took a different view. He felt that it was necessary to industrialize Russia by a crash programme, regardless of suffering or discontent. He reasoned that a war must soon come, and that only an industrialized Russia could face it. In the struggle that followed for control of the Party, the more ruthless man, perhaps inevitably, was able to crush his opponents. In 1929 he launched the first Five-year Plan and the collectivization of Russian agriculture. Russia was forced into the direction which has been followed ever since.

So we may see three main Russian traditions: those of the bureaucrat, the humanist and the theorist. The revolution saw, in principle at any rate, an alliance of the theorist and the humanist against the bureaucrat. But the bureaucrat was not eliminated and alliances shifted until the alignment was of the bureaucrat and the theorist against the humanist. Still, the humanist was by no means destroyed. And in the last few years we have seen a considerable failure of self-confidence on the part of those assembled to suppress him. A section, at least, of the theoreticians has begun to base itself once more on the feelings of the real human being rather than on the millenarian quasi-humanism which fitted in so well with despotism. It is a beginning which the West, without provocative self-righteousness, should do everything in its power to foster.

CHAPTER III

PLANNED ECONOMY

When the first sputnik was thrown into orbit in October, 1957, it was proof of the most visible sort that an extremely advanced technology was operating, and on a big scale, in the Soviet Union. This almost instinctive reaction was certainly right.

It is necessary to get the achievement into perspective. Not even the Russians maintain that the actual state of the Soviet economy at the present moment can be judged simply by this particular triumph. Khrushchev himself made a very apposite remark in his election speech in March, 1958: "We have designed the first artificial earth satellite, but we have not reached the stage of replacing crowbars and spades with machines."

The achievements of Soviet industrialists have been great ones. The engineers and economists in charge of the great expansion which has taken place since the early 'thirties have produced truly phenomenal results, and no one should either detract from their performance or should wish to do so. The scientists and technologists who have put into effect the latest advances, such as the sputniks, the progress in automation and the work on fusion energy, have performed admirably and have deserved the admiration of their colleagues throughout the world. Greatly exaggerated claims and implications have been made for them. But when all the chaff is winnowed, the grain is good and it would be most unfair to think that the process of removing the exaggeration added by a wrong-headed propaganda service, casts any stigma on real Russian achievements.

Russian science has been first-rate since the days of Lomonossov in the eighteenth century. Names like Lobachevsky, Mendeleyev and Pavlov are among the greatest in scientific history. The Soviet achievements in rocketry are tremendously impressive: but it was not that anyone thought that Russian scientists could not measure up to the theoretical work. In fact, as the Russians are glad to point out, the first serious study of the interplanetary rocket was made by the Russian Tsiolkovsky in the early years of this century.

The achievement and the surprise were on a different level. They showed not so much a level of science as a level of technology. In pure science, indeed, the Russians had rather fallen behind in the past generation and most of the achievements in physics and chemistry have until recently been performed in the West. All the theoretical developments of atomic physics originated there, for instance. Even in the last few years all creation of new elements and theoretical and practical detection of new atomic particles have been made in Western Europe and America. But in 1958 Soviet scientists won the Nobel Prize for physics with one important investigation (the Cherenkov effect). And in general their physicists are now at a very high level, as is shown also by their work on thermonuclear power. And, if it comes to that, the explosion by the Russians of a hydrogen bomb some months before the Americans were able to do so was a much more astonishing achievement than their primacy in rocketry.

Yet there is nothing surprising, in a country which has a reasonable supply of scientists at all, about being able to produce these weapons, on one condition: that enough concentration of the scientific and technical resources is made available for the particular projects. The Germans were ten years ahead of the West in rocketry at the end of the war simply because they had decided to allot the necessary resources. The V2 represented an improvement by a factor of more than 100 on the then range and power of rockets, and the Russians made an increase of much the same magnitude, and precisely the same way, though they are not so far ahead of us as the Germans were.

Technically speaking, the main Russian advantage was that they consolidated their programme almost immediately after the end of the war, while in the West it was only taken up seriously three or four years ago. Work in Russia went on continuously in the ensuing period, when the Western powers had abandoned the development. On the other hand, this very concentration probably accounts for the comparatively meagre progress of Soviet science in newer, and so unplannable, fields.

Massive technical advances can be made in modern circumstances only by powers able and willing to concentrate large resources. In Britain, we are inclined to see Soviet achievements in rocketry, say, as representing some sort of general technological superiority, such as produces unhealthy alarm. But it will readily be seen that the case is somewhat different. The Americans, though behind in this particular field, have such a rich economy that, as they have shown, they are capable of providing all the funds that seem necessary for research; sometimes even great individual firms have poured out millions of dollars for such purposes. In Russia the funds have been forthcoming too. It is not that Russia is as rich as the United States or even as Britain. The funds are made available by the ability of the State to cut down on immediate consumption and thus create a great reserve, available for chosen projects.

Where the tax-payer has a reasonably direct say in how the government's money is spent, projects of interest mainly to the State are obviously less easy to finance at the expense of consumer goods. While the Russian sputnik was being launched there were in the Soviet Union 2 million television sets (*Tass*, June 5, 1957) compared to over 40 million in the US. In February, 1959, it was stated at the Party Congress that there were now 3 million. These considerations apply not only to such projects as rocketry, but even more strongly to the whole business of capital investment *versus* consumer goods.

Basically, the economy that ploughs back the largest part of its income into capital investment is going to expand its production most rapidly. At the same time, it is going to have the least to spare for satisfying its population with consumer goods. Other things being equal, it will make the minimal appeal to the voter, with his preference for jam today. And so it is least compatible with political democracy.

This is to put the whole Soviet problem at its broadest. There are other factors. Citizens nowhere insist on having nothing but consumer goods, nor refuse the State and economic leadership *any* capital investment. But at least the voter tends to demand, over any lengthy period, a reasonable division of resources. It might be argued—in fact, it was sometimes argued at the time of the first Five-year Plan—that a socialist proletariat would tighten its belt and forget about incentives, because of its devotion to the cause. This went by the board with the introduction of discriminatory incentives on a wide scale for all higher ranks and of punitive labour discipline for the lower.

The high pressure industrialization and forced collectivization of the early 'thirties represent something quite new, from the point of view of political science. All authorities that involve themselves in economic questions at all are, indeed, interfering, guiding and restricting. But there had not been seen before, at least in modern times, a head-on and total collision between the State and the economic trends.

It was an attempt which, especially on its agricultural

37

side, was thoroughly unpopular. Even the majority of the old Communists, following Bukharin and Rykov, saw no need for it. But the striking point is that a series of schemes justified simply on the grounds of theory were to be enforced.

This is not to make a moral judgement. But it follows, even on Marxist grounds, that the difficulties are immense and can only be overcome by a State machine of sufficient power and discipline to defeat the economic trends, and rulers not only not answerable to the population, but also largely unanswerable to *any* pressures from below: to men possessed by theory and at the same time both ruthless and capable enough to perfect and use the political machinery necessary for such ends.

For Industrialization, the organ of Soviet heavy industry, in its issue of January 1, 1933 stated that the proportion of the Soviet national income allocated to capital development was about 15 per cent in 1929, 30 per cent in 1930 and "already more than 40 per cent" in 1931. These are back-breaking figures. During the First Five-year Plan essential imports were cut back drastically while grain, butter and sugar, already short at home, were exported. In 1931, when there was famine, nearly five million tons of wheat were sold abroad.

Any plan must reconcile requirements with resources, but the first step in Soviet planning in its early years was to draw up a balance sheet of resources to set against already determined requirements. The Goelro plan of 1920 embraced no more than 15 industries; the First Five-year Plan of 1928 prescribed goals for 50 industries and for agriculture. In neither, therefore, could the balances be all-embracing. It was not until 1935 that the State Planning Commission set up sections for co-ordinating the separate balances into a coherent system of balances.

It is a curious feature of the Soviet economy that it has often been obliged to operate without a long-term plan. The First Five-year Plan was approved in April, 1929, six months after it had been due to start. This precedent was repeated in varying degrees in all subsequent plans, until the Sixth Five-year Plan was approved on time in 1956. The Second and Third plans were approved 22 and 14 months late. The Fourth was thrown together in haste and approved by the Supreme Soviet only six months after the Party and the Government had ordered its preparation. "If by a plan is meant a well integrated combination of goals for all, or at least all major economic sectors and factors, the law on the Five-year Plan of Restoration and Development of the National Economy of the USSR in 1946-50 . . . was not a real plan. It was actually an incomplete collection of poorly integrated or entirely unintegrated plans for individual sections of the Soviet economy" (N. Jasny: "A Close-up of the Soviet Fourth Five-year Plan", *Quarterly Journal of Economics*, May, 1952). Even as late as the Fifth Plan comprehensiveness had not been achieved. Baibakov, chief Soviet planner, admitted at the 20th Party Congress in 1956 that for the Fifth Five-year Plan no detailed plan with breakdown by years and by industries had been approved. The Sixth Five-year Plan was the first to be issued within a month of the starting date. It was revised within a year and scrapped within two.

Planners cannot, however extensive their knowledge, predict with accuracy the appearance of new economic and political factors that may affect their calculations over a period as extensive as five years. It was Trotsky who pointed out that only omniscience can devise a total plan.

That Khrushchev's new decentralized planning has not yet attained any greater rigour than the old sort seems to be indicated by a report in *Krokodil* of February 20, 1959. It mentioned three provinces as having changed their capitalization plans fourteen, fifteen and sixteen times respectively in the first eleven months of 1958.

It is clear that a Plan is not, and cannot, be fulfilled precisely. In a thousand fields odd margins of 10% or 20% over-fulfilment are matched by occasional admissions of under-fulfilment. And through the year the fulfilment rates are not even: some industries are ahead in earlier months and slacken off, and it is the opposite with others. Some make use of the way in which their plan is drafted to produce much of an easily manufactured item and little of an equally essential but difficult product. Some managers fake the accounts. Others, staying within the law, produce exaggerations by various means, as Khrushchev complained at some length in his report to the Plenary Session of the Central Committee in June 1959.

All these loose ends and maladjustments must be smoothed out somehow. But no legal method is provided. And so the disproportions of the economy produce considerable economic strains, and are dealt with by means not admitted in the Plan, and not officially tolerated. The economy seeks to find its own level and in spite of all official hindrances manages to do so, though with considerable wastage. Wastages of different types are notorious in other economic systems, including our own. It is difficult to say which are the most deleterious.

There is no difficulty in finding cases of astonishing waste and mismanagement, simply due to bureaucracy, reported from time to time in the Soviet press. For instance, *Pravda* of October 5, 1958, gives an account of a factory which "over many years" has been building useless equipment for garages. Seven million roubles a year are being wasted—"and that is only for the boilers and tyre pumps, without counting the other things".

What is more, *everyone* concerned is well aware of the facts, and wishes to prevent this waste. At the factory, when asked, "Do you know that it is useless in a garage?" they reply,

"Yes, we know. You use the rubber hose to water your gardens, and as for the rest . . . the rubbish dump." But, although the Ministry of Motor Transport, the Scientific Research Institute for Motor Transport, the Distributing Organization, the Chairman of the Gorki Council of National Economy (the new "decentralized" body designed to destroy bureaucratism), the Minister of the Motor and Tractor Industry, the State Planning Commissions of the USSR and of the RSFSR, and various subsidiary bodies, were all as keen as the factory itself to stop the abuse, more than a year had passed in urgent letter-writing and the production of useless equipment, and a new cycle was just starting as *Pravda* went to press.

This sort of thing does not prove for a moment that Soviet industry is lacking in productive dynamism, still less that it is basically unsound. But it does show that the Russian-type planned economy carries a fair margin of that waste and inefficiency which, it was once held, was to have been eliminated with unscientific capitalism.

Another much criticized phenomenon is known as "un-rhythmical working" or "rushing" (*shturmovshchina*). It is really not so much irregular as cyclical, since it takes the form of a regular pile-up of work towards the end of the month. In 1955 Bulganin, describing it as a "major short-coming", instanced three factories in which over 70 per cent of the monthly output was produced in the last ten-day period; and it has persisted since then. The reason normally advanced for this spasmodic working is the late arrival of material or component parts—"disorder in the material-technical supplying of industry", as Bulganin put it. The last months of the year, as well as the last days of the month, are sometimes characterized by a rush of work.

We may take a single case to demonstrate the troubles that can arise at factory level. It is only not typical in that it is rare for so many of the possible troubles to afflict a single factory at once. But all the points mentioned arise with great regularity and are criticized all the time in the Soviet press. It is simply convenient for us to have them, as it were, in one package.

"It seemed to happen suddenly. Last year the factory fulfilled the programme both in respect of gross production and categories of product. Even in the first three months of this year the collective was over-fulfilling the plan. Then suddenly in April there came a collapse. Gross production was only 89·4% of the plan. It is a long time since there was such a setback at the Lenin Building Machinery works in Kharkhov.

"The works administration tried to reassure itself and the workers with talk about the breakdown being an accidental happening. At one of the general factory meetings Comrade Karpukhin, the Chief Engineer, without any economy of glowing terms, described the efforts of the administration to put matters right. But the factory continued to drop back. A new explanation was put forward. It is not our fault, we are being held up by the makers of the electrical equipment.

"But this objective cause, if you can call it that, is not sufficient of itself to explain the failure of the factory. If you had asked us, the workers and foreman, whether the breakdown in April was unexpected, we would have said no. The factory started to work badly last year.

"We might be asked: What do you mean? Surely the plan was fulfilled?

"Yes, it was fulfilled. But at what cost! Rush methods flourish in the factory and they have even recalled people on holiday to the shops. At the same time the factory trade union committee has ceased to show principle and insistence in putting forward and settling the main problems of production and of the working and living conditions of the workers. The obligations undertaken in the collective agreement are systematically disregarded. . . .

"The worker at the machine tool is surrounded by mountains of parts. It is almost impossible to squeeze through between the machines. To get from one machine to another is quite a task.

" 'Yes, it is a bit congested here at the moment,' admits Comrade Shabaltas, the head of the shop, 'but a new crane shop is being built. As soon as it is finished we will spread out into the freed space.'

"When they hear this, the workers only smile grimly. The building of the new shop has been dragging on for 7 years now! . . .

"Is Director Comrade Evsyukov or Chief Engineer Comrade Karpukhin disturbed by the fact that there is no ventilation in the unfinished bay of the foundry? The workers put up with the abnormal conditions, hoping that the building work will be finished soon. . . .

"In the Telpher Shop there is only one welfare room, and that is very small. The trade union organization of the shop passed a resolution to ask the heads of the Telpher and crane shops to move into a joint office, so as to provide a second welfare room. But the administration refused to carry out the suggestion of the trade union organization, and the factory committee, not wanting to spoil relations with the administration, gave no support to the shop committee.

"Last year the factory suffered a loss of 349,000 roubles through wasters, of which 347,000 roubles was due to the foundry.

"Comrade Baitak said: 'We often have to throw out up to 80% of all the parts supplied by the foundry.

43

Because of this we stand idle for 3 to 4 hours every shift.

"Wasters are not our only problem. The situation is no better in regard to tools. An outsider would be very surprised if he could see how milling-machine-operator Ponomarenko is working, for instance. From a distance everything looks all right, but when you come closer you will see that only half a cutter is revolving on the machine. Do not be surprised. Ponomarenko could not get hold of a complete cutter.

"Our machine tool operators cannot get even one-third of their requirements in tools. Out of 100 kinds of cutters needed in the shop, not more than 20 are available. Why? Perhaps there are no castings? It turns out that there are more than sufficient castings. The whole of the trouble is in the organization of output in the tool section. For the last six months the tool section has not once fulfilled the plan, but the factory administration and in particular Comrade Karpukhin are still quite indifferent about it. . . .

"Again it would seem that the factory committee does not want to quarrel with the administration. Between the factory committee and the administration an era of blissful peace has been established. But this peaceful life is bad for the factory. . . .

"The state of affairs in the repair of existing housing accommodation is extremely bad. Here is only one case. The administration provided a room for the newly married Nikolai and Vera Kolesnik. The joy of the newly married couple did not last long. The room turned out to be damp and one wall was covered with mould.

"Kolesnik applied to the factory committee for help in getting the accommodation repaired. Incidentally, the collective agreement provides that the factory committee undertakes to organize constant control over the progress and quality of housing construction, and also the repair of existing buildings. Kolesnik was visited by the chairman of the factory committee, Comrade Filimochuk.

"'Does it leak?' he asked.

"'Like a waterfall. You have to put down bowls and buckets the whole time.'

"'Well, have patience and we will think of something,' promised Filimochuk.

"But he failed to think of anything, and the Kolesnik family, in which a child is now growing up, has been unable to get the promised repairs done for three years now.

"This is not the only case where the factory committee has adopted the bad principle: 'Promise anything now, and later on we will see. . . .'"

Sovietskiye Profsoyuzi, July, 1957.

In the early 'thirties, the capitalist world was going through a terrific economic crisis. In the United States, Britain, Germany and elsewhere the unemployed numbered millions. The economic system appeared not only unjust and inhumane but also inefficient and non-viable.

In 1929 the USSR launched the First Five-year Plan. It was the one country in the world with a state-controlled economy subject to a central plan. And although rumours of serious dislocations and even famines came out, production in general was obviously increasing on the one hand, and and, on the other, unemployment appeared to be unknown.

As completely rigorous proof that the Soviet-type economy was inherently superior to that of the West, this was not indeed sufficient. Even a capitalist economy, if completely cut off from the capitalist economies of the rest of world, might be expected not to have its slumps at the same time as the other countries, particularly if it was going through its first great industrialization boom. And if the Soviet economy

45

avoided the troubles caused by capitalism, that too was not definite proof of its superiority: it might have other troubles. It had no unemployment—but nor had Pharaonic Egypt. The labour camp might be worse than the dole queue.

These objections were indeed made at the time. But it is not difficult to see why many did not heed them. Unemployment was an enormous evil right under our eyes, and it was difficult to imagine that a country without it could be bad in any way, particularly as its own propaganda spoke in the same terms as the humanist socialism of the West and, of course, denied the abuses. Even people who realized the rigours of the Soviet régime felt that these were generally exaggerated, were directed only against obdurate reactionaries, were due largely to local conditions, and in any case were to be regarded as temporary measures—while the victory over economic crises was seen as final and permanent.

That economic crisis can assume catastrophic proportions in a Soviet-type planned economy was made clear by the Polish example.

The Poznan workers' rising (of which Gomulka later said, 'When seizing the weapon of the strike and going out to demonstrate in the street . . . the Poznan workers shouted in a powerful voice "Enough! This cannot go on any longer . . ." ') brought out the truth. Professor Oskar Lange, the régime's leading economist (writing in the fortnightly social-economic magazine, *Życie Gospodarcze*, No. 14, July 16, 1956), first stated what was wrong with Poland's economy. He spoke of 'disproportions' having 'to-day reached a degree which is leading to the disintegration of the national economy'. These disproportions were as follows:

(*a*) 'a disproportion between the development of agriculture and the development of industry'

46

(*b*) 'a disproportion between the production capacity of industry and the supply of materials'

(*c*) 'a disproportion between the development of industrial production in quantity and quality, and also in operating costs'

(*d*) 'a disproportion between capital investment and production programmes, and the obsolete technological state of many factories'.

'These disproportions are demonstrated by great difficulties in our foreign trade; by a lack of reserves of materials, causing delays in production and a failure to utilize the existing production capacity of industry; by the wastage of raw and other materials; by the bad and hardly functioning system of supply to the population. On the basis of these disproportions arose the most important disproportion: a disproportion between the powerful growth of the forces of production and the weak improvement of the living standard of the people. This caused the non-fulfilment of the Six-year Plan in the sphere of raising the living standard of the people, in the sphere constituting the social justification of building socialism.'

He went on to say that this had resulted in 'a growing indifference to work' with 'a paralysing effect on our daily life'. 'Moral and political appeals and legal and administrative orders' had exhausted their possibilities. The working class had lost interest and this in turn caused poor workmanship and wastefulness.[1] And in general, he said, 'immediate action is needed to halt and avert the growing process of the disintegration of the national economy'.

Strong words. And within a few weeks events had shown them to be no stronger than the case deserved. Gomulka, in

[1] Poor workmanship in many British industries, it may be noted in passing, has been attacked by observers here during the last decade or so. (V.G.)

47

his speech to the Central Committee of October 20, 1956, revealed that the credit system was that of 'an insolvent bankrupt'; that huge, useless factories had been built; that coal production was below the 1949 level; that less than half of the housing plan had been fulfilled; that, in spite of subsidies and preferential treatment, collective farms had 'smaller results and greater production costs' than individual farms; and that the claim that wages had increased 27% during the Six-year Plan was a falsehood. The Polish example shows, in an extreme form, that state planning, on the basis of the theories of Marxism-Leninism, has no inherent superiority over any other economic system. This is by no means to say that it cannot work, and still less to judge between it and pure capitalism on ethical grounds, one way or the other: it is simply to say that it is as liable to defects of a catastrophic nature as any other system.

Agriculture is one of the spheres in which the Soviet régime has found its most intractable problems. The aim of securing maximum production is often in conflict with the aim of turning the peasant into an employee. Oscillations, compromises and sudden drastic changes in policy are frequent.

Moreover, it is a sphere, above all others, where results depend in a large measure on an uncontrollable phenomenon—the weather. A bad crop is a major factor in the struggle for power, for it is usual to blame it, in part at least, on the incompetence of those in control. A good crop makes the *status quo* easier to maintain.

According to Stalin, a distinguishing feature of collectivization was that it was carried out "from above, on the initiative of the State" (*Short History of the Communist Party*, Moscow, 1943). Collectivization was designed to increase the efficiency of Soviet agriculture and to release manpower for the new industries. Instead of being farmed in private plots, the land was to be operated in common, and the large farms thus created would receive from industry machinery which would be uneconomic in the small private farms. At the same time, it was hoped, the incorrigible private property-mindedness of the individual peasant would give way under the re-education of co-operative life.

None of these things happened. First of all, Stalin's method of collectivization involved obtaining the support of the poor peasants and the benevolent neutrality of the medium peasants. In the process the richer peasants, the kulaks, were to be eliminated. This last part went through according to plan, and some ten million peasants either died or were deported. But the non-kulak peasant masses showed no enthusiasm at all and after a year of famine and agricultural disruption, during which almost all the peasantry had been forced into collective farms, the Government faced a crisis in the villages. In the interests of the next harvest, it was forced to relax.

Although the relaxation was by no means complete, two-thirds of the collectivized peasantry took advantage of it to leave the collective farms.

Over the next few years economic pressures of a less violent nature were put upon them and they were gradually starved back into the kolkhozes. But they had won one major concession; each was permitted to keep a private plot and one or two cattle. These footholds of private property have been far more productive than the collective farms—even in 1957 private cattle produced more than half the meat and milk of the USSR—and they have been used by peasants to negate as far as possible the effects of collectivization. It is only now that there is some real threat, as apart from talk, of suppressing them.

From a production point of view, too, the collectives were not a success. The 1928 level was not reached again until the 'fifties. Only five to six years ago it was revealed by

49

Khrushchev (in his reports of the plenary meetings of the Party Central Committee in September, 1953, and February, 1954) that the amount of grain *per capita*, and of cattle absolutely, was less than it had been in Tsarist times. Moreover, the expected release of manpower did not take place. Even now, the rural working population of the Soviet Union is much the same as it was in 1928. The industrial working class has grown and taken up the population increase, but, with all the mechanization and so on, much the same manpower is required on the land to produce the same results as when the backward moujik farmed his little plot.

As Khrushchev has complained, the efficiency in terms of labour of American agriculture is incomparably ahead of that of Russia; depending on what figures one takes, the British or American farmer is from six to twelve times more productive than his Soviet equivalent.

Over the last two decades the proportion of the manpower on the land has dropped from three-fifths to about two-fifths but it is still roughly the same as it was in Western Europe 60/70 years ago.

The basic difficulty of the kolkhoz system was given particularly clearly, as late as the December, 1958, meeting of the Central Committee, in the following exchange:

Mustafaev I.D. (Secretary of the Azerbaijan Central Committee): "Nevertheless an enormous quantity of cattle in the private sector consumes a great deal of people's time; a great deal of the fodder resources of the kolkhozes is expended."

Khrushchev: "The kolkhoz cattle is being embezzled."

Mustafaev: "We have checked in the kolkhozes. In individual kolkhozes payment has been levied for pasturing cattle. . . . It is true that when this question was discussed in many kolkhozes they did not agree with this and decided to pasture the cattle free."

Khrushchev: "Comrade Mustafaev, we do not object to re-organization of the countryside. But you are introducing an incorrect proposal. In essence you are proposing to lay down a tribute. But the countryside must be reconstructed on socialist principles. What you are talking about is a tax; this is a policy of fines; it does not suit us. Educative work must be carried on among the population. In the first place, Communists who work in the countryside must set a real example. Attention must be paid to this. Otherwise cattle-owners will pay a tax, buy themselves off and develop private livestock rearing, and it will be difficult to improve the collective side. The facts of which you speak are evidence of weakness in education of the kolkhozniks and even of Communists."

Mustafaev: "True, Nikita Sergeevich; time is needed to make use of the opportunity."

Khrushchev: "What time is needed? Forty-one years of Soviet power, a sufficient period, has passed."

Mustafaev: "We have not made use of our opportunity yet. I agree with your reply. . . ."

At the Plenary Session of the Polish Communist Central Committee held in October, 1956, Gomulka brought out the economic truths about a collective farm system run on Soviet lines. He pointed out that in 1955 individual farms had produced 16·7% more per hectare than collectives and 37% more than State farms. To keep agricultural collectives solvent, their compulsory deliveries of produce to the State had been deliberately postponed since December, 1955; these arrears alone were worth 500 million zlotys. In addition, credits totalling 2,500 million zlotys had been pumped into the collectives, and artificial fertilizer had been supplied to them to the extent of 58·6 kilograms per hectare—individual peasants received half this amount. Despite this, the individual farms had produced a fifth more per hectare than the collectives, where costs were rising and production constantly falling.

When Gomulka made them voluntary, within months over 80% of the collectives disintegrated and the peasants returned to individual farming.

The Soviet long-term plan for the collective farms is to merge them and transform them into something resembling the state farms, which now form a minority of all farms.

It was stated in Khrushchev's theses for the Seven Year Plan that the collective farmer's productivity will have to go up 200 per cent during that period, whereas his standard of living is to rise by only 40 per cent. He is to be weaned from his private plot. Collective farmers in general, following the example of Kalinovka, Khrushchev's birthplace, are "voluntarily" to yield up their acres and cattle to the communal sector and to purchase their milk, meat and vegetables from the farm.

Khrushchev's "virgin lands" campaign launched in 1954 was on the basis of state farms. There were many objections to the programme, and in the long run most independent experts seem to feel that the soil on these marginal areas will become exhausted unless very uneconomic amounts of capital are poured into them continuously. Meanwhile, they have given good harvests (except in 1957) and they serve as pilots for the eventual centralization of agriculture. The only question is whether such a centralization will be possible without at least as great upsets as those produced when Stalin launched his attack on the individual peasantry.

At the 21st Communist Party Congress in January, 1959, a new economic plan, this time a Seven-year one, was launched with much enthusiasm. It replaces the Sixth Five-year Plan, scaled down at the end of 1956 and abandoned in 1957, since when no Plan had been in operation.

52

The main themes of the new Plan are the catching up with the USA, or rather with the present production of the USA in certain industrial products, on the one hand, and the equalling of Western meat and milk production on the other. "Catching up with the United States" has long been a Soviet aim. In 1931 it was said that this should be done by 1941. In 1939 it was "in the immediate future". In 1946 it was "soon" and in 1956 it was hoped to attain it in the early 1960's. At present Soviet milk and meat production *per capita* is not only less than a third of American and about a quarter of Danish production, but is even below countries like Britain where only a small proportion of the population is engaged in agriculture and where the economy is based on the large-scale importation of food.

Farm output is supposed to rise at 8 per cent per year. The grain target of 180 million tons, fixed originally for 1960, has now been postponed until 1965. As the meat target for 1960, intended to bring the Soviet citizen within reach of American consumption, was pegged to the grain figure, meat and live-stock plans have had to be slowed down too.

There are all sorts of obvious traps about comparing production figures and rates of increase between one country and another. It has been pointed out by Western economists that all economic statistics beyond a mere statement of the bulk produced in actual tonnage in particular industries involve some form of value judgement. For many years Soviet statistics were a particularly difficult field, since ordinary production figures were never given, but only percentages based on earlier production calculated in a quite unreal fashion in 1926 prices. All that needs to be said is that a good many assumptions and twists could be and were smuggled in and the figures can be regarded as virtually meaningless. It is difficult to sort out what true, or at any rate reasonable, figures would be as against the great

53

improvements claimed. But in the comparable case of Poland, where it had been stated that wages had improved by 27% during the post-war Six-year Plan, Gomulka revealed in his speech of October 20, 1956, that no increase at all had in fact taken place.

In the last couple of years Soviet statistics have greatly improved. A great deal of confusion and miscalculation still exists, but actual production figures are now available for many sections of the economy. It is true that some attempt was made to combine these new and presumably reasonably accurate tonnages with the old and certainly phoney grand claims. For these last continue to be made, as in Khrushchev's speech to the 21st Party Congress. But Soviet economists have found themselves faced with a number of difficulties. For instance, it is officially claimed that between 1913 and 1957 industrial production in the present USSR increased 33 times, while in the USA it only increased 5 times. Allowing for population differences Ostrovityanov, the leading Soviet economist, stated that the present discrepancy between *per capita* production of the two countries is five times smaller than it was in 1913. Soviet economists also state that in 1913 Russian production was *per capita* 21·4 times smaller than the American. If these two contentions are put together, it follows that Soviet *per capita* output would now be a quarter of that of the US. But the claim actually made is that Soviet production *per capita* is now almost half that of the US. Something is clearly wrong. And the only way out is either to admit that pre-Soviet Russia was not as backward as is maintained, or that the US is still further ahead than is claimed. In either case the Soviet rate of increase is not as high as is frequently said. Some Soviet economists have started to revise their estimates of pre-revolutionary production, in which they are undoubtedly correct. They have not yet gone on to revise the hitherto alleged Soviet rate of increase, but doubtless this will come.

It is difficult to get a figure for the Soviet national income. In April, 1957 a Soviet economist, O. T. Bogomolov, stated that Soviet exports amounted to 3 per cent of the national income; and that the total of exports plus imports was 25 thousand million "currency" roubles. Exports and imports balance approximately and the "currency rouble" is defined as quarter of a dollar. This would give a national income of 109 thousand million dollars—i.e. about 505 dollars a head. The 1955 *per capita* national income in dollars for the USA was 2,027, and for the United Kingdom 1,284.

Soviet economists have found propaganda methods of computation a nuisance to them when they want to find out what is really happening. They even call for the estimates of Soviet and Western production to be made on the basis of "comparable prices" (*Planned Economy*, No. 6, 1956). Writing in "*Kommunist*" in 1959, Academician Nemchinov warned against certain illusions about the Soviet Union achieving superiority over the capitalist world at the end of the Seven-year Plan. He said that in 1965 production of energy in Soviet Russia per head of population would still be below the present output level of the USA, Canada, Britain, Belgium and Sweden. Nemchinov also stated that in 1965 Russia would produce approximately one motor-car for every 1,000 inhabitants. In Britain the present level of annual production is one car per 70 inhabitants. Such realistic assessments did not find their way into the discussion at the Congress itself.

The prospects of fulfilling the plan as it stands seem dubious. Most independent experts appear to regard the agricultural figures as unreal but most of the industrial aims as at least possible. The main query in industry is whether it will be feasible, as planned, to increase Soviet labour productivity at the annual rate of 9% (*Trud*, 22 Jan. 1959).

It has averaged 7·3% over the past seven years and is decreasing, in accordance with the diminishing returns natural in the circumstances. If this proves a hindrance the plan might still be put through, but at the expense of all the benefits supposed to accrue to the worker.

Soviet claims are undoubtedly exaggerated: but it would be foolish to deduce from this that their economic achievements are small. The plans in operation at a given moment may be unlikely to be fulfilled as intended: the general claims about overtaking the US if the plans *are* fulfilled may be propagandist: yet this is not to say that very striking and important progress is unlikely, or to deny that, in some spheres, it has actually taken place. It is only too easy to imagine that the exposure of a boast as exaggerated means that we may write off even very partial fulfilment. The economy can be distinguished from the propaganda. The nature of the propaganda is of interest in showing the type of exhortation and justification the political leadership thinks required. But meanwhile the factories are really working, the engineers are at their design boards, and capital investment is being kept to a high rate. Leaving aside the claims, it is also true that the Soviet economy has many unadmitted faults. But these are not such as to prevent an expansion, and a rapid one.

Yet although the plan in a number of respects seems to be both feasible and admirable, it is at present, on the whole, a matter of intention rather than of reality: and recent difficulties with it have been so great that these, rather than its potentialities, must impinge as being the more substantial. The reasons, however, we must give it the greatest attention are that it represents, up to a point at least, the possible economic future of the Soviet Union, and in any case it is the theme which will dominate Soviet internal attitudes for many years.

CHAPTER IV

THE POLITICAL BACKGROUND

THIS IS NOT a Handbook to the Soviet Union. Such a work would deal with such formal documents as the Constitution, and with the State structure, at some length. All that need be said on this side of things is that the constitution is one guaranteeing all the democratic liberties as known in the West, providing for the minority nationalities a highly developed system of autonomy, and setting up a method of governing the country based on the Supreme Soviet, a body elected by universal suffrage and ruling the State in much the same way as the parliaments with which the West is familiar.

Since it is not the formalities but the realities which we are dealing with, to approach matters from this end would be mistaken. What is necessary is to look at the actual activities, and it can then be seen whether the descriptions fit.

There can be little comparison between the powers of the Supreme Soviet and those of a Western parliament. The length of its sessions indicates some of the difference. In 1955 it sat for fourteen days; in 1956 for five; in 1957 for fifteen; and in 1958 for nine. In between times it is represented by its Presidium which issues decrees later ratified by the Supreme Soviet itself. And even the Presidium is simply a body ratifying decisions of the Party. This was shown, for example in the expulsion of Malenkov, Molotov and the "anti-party group" from the Central Committee in June, 1957. This was followed instantly by their dismissal from their government posts by a decree of the Presidium of the Supreme Soviet, ratified by the Supreme Soviet proper on December 20. There has never been an instance of the Supreme Soviet rejecting any decree issued by this Presidium.

In 1957 the main session of the Supreme Soviet lasted from February 5 to February 12. On February 5 procedural matters were laid before both chambers and adopted unanimously. On February 6-9 both chambers adopted the—highly controversial—economic measures, then at issue. In one chamber, the Soviet of Nationalities, there were thirty-two speeches and the plan and budget were approved unanimously. Seven more resolutions and legislative proprosals of some importance were adopted between February 9 and the end of the session. Twenty-one more speeches were made and all proposals were adopted unanimously. The speakers gave the impression of being complementary, each presenting some particular aspect of the Party's proposals. Foreign affairs, for example, might have aroused some qualms about official policy in view of the events of 1956 in Eastern Europe. In fact only eleven speeches were made, as unanimously favourable as the vote itself. An article in *Sovetskaya Rossiya* of February 26, 1957, commented that deputies to the Supreme Soviet had not delivered any opposition speeches in the past and would not deliver them in the future.

It can be deduced that the constitutional arrangements of the USSR are not, at present, of the slightest real significance. We should seek the realities of rule, and of power, elsewhere.

The struggle for real power in the Soviet Union often provides the world public with dramatic events. Among the serious-minded there is a tendency to regard it all as slightly vulgar. It is held that the important side of Soviet life lies in the great social tides which, though not producing eye-catching phenomena at a superficial level, are yet in the long run all that matter. This does not seem to be quite right.

For where the State is so organized as to be an Archimedean lever by which a few individuals can exert as much social power as whole classes, the norms of sociology and of political theory apply rather badly. Tolstoy saw this when he said that what he most greatly feared was a Genghiz Khan with a telephone. In Poland, Radio Sczeczyn in November, 1956, gave an account of the Stalinist attempt to overthrow Gomulka. A copy of the plan of the Stalinist group to seize power had been accidently passed to an official of the Security Forces who was not on their side, so that it was possible to take steps to thwart them. On such individual incidents do the fates of whole régimes depend. One might consider this type of rule quite simply as an apparatus for rendering the social forces inoperative, or as a machine for overcoming the materialist forces of history as seen by Marx, and imposing on them the ideas of a ruling group: for creating conditions to which an idealist conception of history for once largely applies.

There is nothing sinister in the emergence of faction at policy-making levels in the USSR. However rigid in appearance the ideology, however centralized the State, problems must present themselves continually which are capable of two or more solutions. It is perfectly clear that problems of this sort have actually arisen in the USSR and that different leaders have offered different solutions.

Stalin's methods of dealing with political opponents are now, by admission, known to have consisted of destroying them physically. The tradition was established that an alternative policy to Stalin's was not simply less acceptable, but led logically and automatically to counter-revolution and to the participation of its advocates in plots against the State and in favour of imperialist intervention. The struggle between policies was thus linked to a very particular technique in the struggle for power. And, although the theory of a monolithic party was maintained in public, it became perfectly plain that a contender for power required a powerful faction of supporters to put in positions where they could provide the necessary control of the Party machinery, or of Police machinery capable of dominating that of the Party.

We can distinguish several phases in Stalin's rise to despotic power. First came the series of manœuvres which drove the other leading figures from office. Stalin plus Zinoviev and |Kamenev, plus the "Rightists" Bukharin and Rykov, eliminated Trotsky. Then Stalin, plus Bukharin and Rykov, eliminated the Zinoviev-Kamenev group. Then Stalin got rid of Bukharin and the Rightists. Thus by the early 'thirties Stalin had complete control of the leading Party organs. So far the contest had been simply political and no repressive action was taken against the opposition except for the expulsion of Trotsky from the country. Stalin had won largely by using his position as General Secretary to organize the voting for Congresses. But he also relied on the support of a number of fairly important figures who agreed with him on policy grounds.

In 1934 Stalin held his "Congress of Victors", which was almost entirely composed of his own men. The next phase was the destruction of those of his supporters who simply agreed with him on political grounds and were not willing just to accept orders (particularly in not going through with the execution of the opposition). These, including the great majority of the "Victors", were themselves eliminated. But while the oppositionists were mostly shot after public trial, the moderate Stalinists were simply not heard of again. By 1938-9 Stalin had put through this second purge and the leadership consisted of men of proved reliability from his point of view. They included both Khrushchev and his recent rivals.

After the war a series of struggles developed among Stalin's subordinates. And this is probably relevant to the present period; for it signifies that even if Khrushchev establishes a completely solid personal control like Stalin's, it is not likely to prevent a bitter rivalry among his lieutenants.

Malenkov had become Stalin's most powerful lieutenant by 1946, but during that and the following year Zhdanov came to the fore with a much more intransigeant policy both in foreign affairs and in bringing Soviet life under ideological control. At the same time a rather similar struggle was being fought out in the Ukraine between Kaganovich and Khrushchev. Zhdanov's policies came to grief in 1948 with the failure to discipline Tito. He died in August, 1948, and within a few months his allies were removed from their posts throughout the Party and the State. In 1949-50 a large number of them were tried and shot in the so-called "Leningrad Case", already referred to.

Thenceforward Malenkov was invariably named as No. 2 to Stalin, while Khrushchev was brought back from the Ukraine to balance him on the Party Secretariat. In the ensuing years there were several signs of tension, including attacks on Khrushchev's agricultural proposals by associates in the Caucasus of the Police chief, Beria.

At the end of 1951 there came a new phase, with the arrest of a number of Beria's men in Georgia on accusations of nationalism. At about the same time the Ministry of State Security passed out of the hands of his nominees. In the early part of 1952 the Georgian purge continued. In August a group of Jewish politicians and writers were shot in the "Crimean Affair". In October, at the 19th Party Congress, Stalin had a new and much larger body named to lead the Party—the "Presidium", which replaced the old Politburo.

His intention, as Khrushchev has since told us, was to get rid of his old subordinates and replace them by new men. Those certainly under attack included Molotov, Mikoyan, Beria and Voroshilov. Those destined to fill their places included such members of Khrushchev's present Presidium as Aristov, Brezhnev and Ignatov. In January, 1953 it was announced that a group of doctors, mainly Jewish, had been arrested on charges including the murder of Zhdanov. Every indication was that Stalin was intending to start again, and if anything on an even more violent scale, the great purges of the 'thirties. In March, 1953, he died and the old leaders regained control, Beria in particular notably strengthening his position. Within the month Beria's Ministry announced that the doctors' plot and the parallel Georgian conspiracies were frame-ups, and Malenkov, at first holding both Stalin's positions as head of the Government and leading Party Secretary, was forced to give up the Secretaryship.

In June Beria was arrested by his colleagues, to be shot in December.

For the next four years a complex and bitter struggle took place among the surviving leaders. We have only lately obtained much evidence in the way of official statements about this. But it can be seen that Khrushchev first attacked Malenkov, removing him from the Premiership in February, 1955, and then turned on Molotov. In February, 1956, Khrushchev launched his repudiation of Stalin. There seems no doubt that in one aspect at least this was connected with the struggle for power: Khrushchev used the curious expression that the denunciation of Stalin did not imply a "mutual amnesty" between his successors. But at the time he was unable to secure any change in the Presidium. A stalemate ensued. The events of 1956, which included the Hungarian Revolution and the coming to power of Gomulka in Poland, together with the collapse of the Sixth Five-year Plan, greatly weakened Khrushchev's position. He retrieved lost ground early in 1957 and made the running with proposals for the decentralization of industry. But things hardened against him among his colleagues, and in June, 1957, they struck for power. It has since been made clear officially that the majority of the Presidium voted Khrushchev down. They calculated, their opponents now say, that a resolution presented in the name of the Presidium would be accepted by the Central Committee. But the anti-Khrushchev forces did not remain solid under the pressures brought against them by the Party apparatus, the Police, and the Army headed by Zhukov. Khrushchev was able to expel Molotov, Malenkov and Kaganovich, and fill the Presidium with his own supporters.

Depending on the Army was a dangerous thing, and once his main opponents were defeated Khrushchev turned on Zhukov and expelled him, re-establishing Party control in the armed forces. During the following year he dealt with those leaders who had supported Malenkov and Molotov but given way in the crisis. Bulganin was removed from the Premiership (which Khrushchev himself took), and was later denounced; and in January, 1959 Pervukhin and Saburov were also publicly censured.

These are merely the main lines of an immensely complicated series of manœuvres. The rate of wastage among the leadership may be seen by examining the Presidium which took over on Stalin's death in 1953. There were 10 full and 4 candidate members. Of these 14, 2 have been shot and 7 removed from their positions under grave political charges. One of the others has been quietly dropped. In addition 2 of those promoted in the interim period to fill gaps have also been expelled with obloquy.

It is impossible to sort out motives in a struggle of this kind. If we ask to what extent Khrushchev's decentralization of industry in 1957 was motivated by a desire to give the Party apparatus which he controlled a grip on positions hitherto held by his adversaries, and how far he was sincerely motivated by a desire to rid Soviet industry of some of its bureaucratic excrescences, we are probably asking a meaningless question and one which he himself would be unable to answer.

In dealing with the actual methods used in the struggle for power, at least during Stalin's time, we are looking at an example of the worst in Soviet life. Enough of the facts are, since Khrushchev's Secret Speech, beyond dispute and the story of terror, torture and murder carried out, in this case not against political opponents in the ordinary sense, but against colleagues and collaborators on the one hand and innocent bystanders like the doctors on the other, is a shocking one. Awareness of occasional Western outrages, especially in Africa, should not tempt us to palliate terror as a regular method of government.

The present régime has expressed its intention of ending this type of thing. And the Soviet people are so sensitive and so hostile to any idea of a renewal of the terror that it would not be easy to begin again on the old lines. Nevertheless, only a few weeks after Khrushchev's speech another former candidate member of the Presidium, Mir Dzhaffar Bagirov, went before the firing squad. What is more, the execution of this important figure was not announced in the central Press, but only in the local Baku paper, and that a month after the event. In 1958 Imre Nagy and his associates, who had been kidnapped by the Soviet Security Police in spite of a safe conduct, were executed. To doubt the ruthlessness of the present rulers, when they feel that ruthlessness is politically advantageous, would be therefore quite unrealistic.

Yet if we compare Khrushchev's position with that of Stalin in the early 'thirties, we can see certain obvious differences, quite apart from the facts that Khrushchev is no Stalin and that he is twenty years older than Stalin was. The first difference, and one of high importance, is the strength of feeling, depth of experience, the hopes and the education of the Soviet people. The second is the fact that the present Central Committee membership consists of men whose political life has taught them not to take survival on trust. The third is probably crucial: it does not seem, at present at least, that Khrushchev's economic schemes are likely to produce quite as violent stresses as those pursued by Stalin. If this turns out to be incorrect, we may perhaps see some renewal of the terror: for, public sentiment apart, no change has taken place in the actual structure of Soviet authority to prevent the Stalinist system from being clamped down once again.

In looking closely at the methods pursued in Stalin's time, we are, in any case, not dealing with distant history. It was during that period that the present leadership came to the fore and gained its experience. Khrushchev himself held high posts, rising to the top during the terror as a substitute for the executed Postyshev; and similarly with the senior members of the present Presidium. The junior members came up during the bitter time of the late 'forties and are of similar background. Aristov, for instance, was the Central Committee Secretary in charge of Party Organization during the Doctors' Plot period. In considering future possibilities, therefore, it could be imprudent to overlook, as one factor in the situation, the background of training which the present leadership received in two spheres particularly— the attitude to human life and the attitude to truth. It must be remembered, at the same time, that this is one factor only.

Khrushchev's disavowal of Stalin exposed the whole unpleasantness of the former régime. He has since, as a result of the failure of the attempt to obtain rule by consent in 1956, gone back to a considerable extent on his words. He and his colleagues were indeed in an awkward position. It had proved difficult for them to manage the Communist world while they were still held responsible for Stalin's narrow brutality and yet lacked his authority. But the attempt to disavow him resulted in even greater difficulties. So an attempt had to be made to put Humpty Dumpty, in some degree, together again. "Anti-Stalinism" was condemned as an attempt to sow discord. Stalin was again described as "a great Communist", and Khrushchev enthusiastically proclaimed himself a disciple of the dead dictator.

But even at the time of the strongest assault on Stalin, in the Secret Speech of February, 1956, his attacks had not been without reservation. He had said: "You see to what Stalin's mania for greatness led. He had completely lost touch with reality." He had spoken of Stalin's agricultural plans as based on no facts or figures, since "a genius does not need to count". He had shown him as approving "loathsome adulation", and personally ordering beatings of prisoners. He had seen fit, on the other hand, to maintain that Stalin was not a "giddy despot", but looked at matters "from the position of the interest of the working class", to call him "one of the strongest Marxists", and to praise his "logic, strength and will".

This ambivalence leads to very peculiar results. We are told that in Stalin's Russia it was possible for all power to become concentrated in the hands of one man, and he an irresponsible monster; that he perpetrated massacres of all political figures opposed to him; that he ordered the deportation of entire nations; that he was able to impose thoroughly disastrous decisions in economic matters which he did not understand. At the same time we are told that the Soviet society of his day was a "Socialist" one in which the workers ruled. This means, at the very best to define

Socialism in a purely mechanistic way, and to rob it of what could be recognized by its supporters and its opponents alike as its spirit.

It is most interesting, moreover, to note Khrushchev's general attitude to terrorism as such, even in the Secret Speech. His main denunciation of Stalin is for directing terror against his own accomplices. Apart from this he is concerned only with the terror against loyal Army officers, and the mass deportations of some, but not all, of the national minorities who suffered in this way. It will be seen that there are considerable omissions. It is nowhere implied that it is not perfectly legitimate to massacre non-Communists. On the contrary, Lenin is invoked as having "without hesitation used the most extreme methods against enemies". Stalin is condemned for using "physical annihilation not only against actual enemies"; and, above all, the largest scale of all Stalin's terror operations—against the mass of the Russian peasantry—is passed over with praise for agricultural collectivization.

Again, Khrushchev virtually confines his attack on the Yezhov terror to its effect on the top ranks of the Party, the odd thousands of whose execution Stalin personally approved. It must be remembered, however, that the terror affected the population on a mass scale. It has been estimated that there were about seven million arrests in the years 1937 and 1938, and the late Mosha Pijade, one of the leaders of the Yugoslav Communists, estimated in a speech on August 6, 1951, that more than three million people had actually been killed.

Look, again, at Khrushchev's attitude to an intermediate class—"deviationist" communists. It is an ambiguous one. He implies that Stalin ordered the Kirov murder; but he does not explicitly exonerate Zinoviev, who was shot for it. (Nor do more recent Soviet histories clear up the matter: on the contrary those appearing in 1959 present a more than ordinarily misleading combination of *suppressio veri* and *suggestio falsi*.) Khrushchev asks whether it was "necessary to annihilate" people who "broke with Trotskyism and returned to Leninist positions"; but this is rather different to pleading for Trotskyites proper. He defines the political line of the oppositionists as leading "actually toward the restoration of capitalism and capitulation to the world bourgeoisie", which seems to make them "enemies". On the other hand, he notes with approval that "during the progress of the furious ideological fight . . . extreme repressive measures were not used against them". Perhaps this uncertain attitude is best summed up in the carefully qualified phrase, "in regard to those persons who in their time had opposed the Party line, there were often no sufficiently serious reasons for the physical annihilation". If this is what is felt, even twenty years later, about "companions of Lenin", it is natural enough that Khrushchev does not conceal his approval of "extreme measures" against non-Communists.

Khrushchev's denunciation of Stalin removed the last disguise from the fact that the Communist world had been ruled by fiat from the top. And though Stalin's particular crimes were denounced, there has been no reorganization to prevent power accumulating as before in the hands of one or a few men. Moreover, it is not simply a question of Stalin. Khrushchev's speech asserted that *all* Lenin's companions and successors had deviated from his views: Bukharin and Trotsky, Rykov and Zinoviev, and now Stalin. Nor, even officially, could it be said that the rulers on whom Stalin's mantle had fallen were the sort of people that any properly run party should have elected or reelected. Malenkov and Molotov, Kaganovich, Bulganin and Beria, were all revealed as having plotted to seize power

contrary to the interests of the people. It is true that Khrushchev maintains that they failed because they lack support.
But there are few even in the Communist Parties who do
not feel that the opposite is true—they lack support because
they failed:

'Treason doth never prosper. What's the reason?
For if it prosper, none dare call it treason.'

"At least Khrushchev is not like Stalin. He removes his
opponents peacefully and does not kill them." Statements
like this have been made quite frequently about the recent
purges in the Soviet Union. They are based on a misunderstanding—of Stalin.

For he too took peaceful action against his opponents at
first. From 1923 to 1926, he carried on, as Khrushchev did
from 1953 for a similar period, a struggle against his opponents in the Politburo based on political argument and
intrigue. It was only in 1926 that Stalin obtained a majority
in the Politburo. From 1926 to 1930 he used this majority
until in the latter year he had rid the Politburo of anyone
who had ever opposed him on any issue. Khrushchev has
not reached that position.

The immediate fate of Stalin's main opponents after their
fall from the centre of power was not more illiberal than that
which has befallen Molotov and Co. After Kamenev, for
instance, was removed from the Politburo in 1926, he became
Ambassador to Italy. He was expelled from the Party in
1927, but readmitted in 1928 and made Director of the
Supreme Council of National Economy. He was expelled
from the Party again in 1932, but readmitted the same year.
And it was only in 1935 that he was sentenced to imprisonment and in the following year to death. Similarly with
others: Bukharin, "expelled" from the Politburo and Central

Committee in 1929, held various posts and was Editor of *Izvestia* from 1934 until 1937, the year before his execution. Rykov, the Prime Minister, expelled from the Politburo and the Party in 1929, became a Party member again in 1931 and was Commissar of Communications from then until 1937. He was executed in 1938.

Thus everything that can be said about Khrushchev's moderation now could have been said about Stalin at the comparable period.

Of course, none of this proves in any way that Khrushchev has an intention of reintroducing the old style terror. It only shows that his record so far is little different from Stalin's; and if Khrushchev has spoken adversely of purges, so did Stalin in 1925, when he described as shocking the idea that members of the opposition should even be removed from the Politburo. A perhaps hopeful point, however, may be noted. The removal of Molotov, Malenkov and Co. was accompanied by public references to crimes which they had committed in the course of their Stalinist duties: the Leningrad frame-up of 1949 in Malenkov's case, and the great purge of 1938 in the cases of Molotov and Kaganovich. When these charges were made in public speeches by Khrushchev himself and a minority of the victors, the implication was that the First Secretary wished to proceed at once to extremes. That the charges have not been followed up seems to imply that he has been blocked by his own supporters—as, for the matter of that, Stalin was in 1932.

For the present, then, there is an improvement. In certain circumstances, it may well be consolidated and even extended. Yet to ignore the political background would be the act of an ostrich. While it cannot be excluded for a moment that the present leaders have had a definite change of ideas about methods of rule, it might be safer to rely on such pressures as may exist to keep them in line in the matter.

This means, in the long run, on the Soviet people, and points to the importance of utilizing any opportunity of making genuine contact with them.

My intention in this chapter has been to illustrate as clearly as possible the *differences* between Soviet political life and that which most people in the West are used to. For it is of the greatest importance that anyone trying to understand what is going on in the USSR should keep up continually the imaginative effort of holding his mind fully tuned to Soviet attitudes. It is only too easy to find oneself unconsciously slipping into habits of thought due simply to an upbringing in a different society—democratic reflexes, as it were—whose expectations seem to carry the sanction of "common sense". (This is perhaps made even easier by the Soviet use of political expressions similar to those we are all used to, and even to institutional arrangements formally resembling, and sometimes with the same titles as, Western equivalents.)

Even now, one often sees writing on Soviet political themes which are based on adequate information, and to which reasonable thought has been applied, but which are yet practically worthless because of this imaginative failure.

CHAPTER V

STATE AND PEOPLE

THE SOVIET STATE and Party impinge on the population in three main ways: in their conditions of living, where
the State is responsible for the organization of the economy;
in their conditions of thought, in that the State directly or
indirectly prescribes the information and culture which will
be available to citizens; and in direct action through the
laws and instruments of compulsion.

All three derive from the government's conviction that it
knows what is best for the citizen in every sphere and in
every respect.

The compulsive aspect of the Soviet State is for many
people in the West its most obvious side. When the Soviet
Union is described as a "police state" it is this that people
have in mind—the stereotype of a vast apparatus of terror,
unrestricted by legal or any other considerations.

During the worst times this side of Soviet affairs hardly
differed from the most unpleasant ideas that were held about
it. The crushing of the independent peasants in the early
'thirties resulted in at least the five million deaths which
Stalin told Churchill had been necessary. The 1936-8
"period of mass repression", as it is now called, produced
similar casualties. In the Party itself purges were almost
continuous from the time Stalin sent the first Party members
to the execution cellars in 1936 up to the moment of his
death when the great new purge, centred on the Doctors'
Plot, was in preparation.

The scale of the great purges says sufficient about the

power of the Police at its height. With Beria's execution in 1953 the Police was brought under Party control. The attacks on police excesses won widespread support from the population and pressure to prevent them in future became strong.

The Soviet Union has the largest militarized police force in the world, estimated at about half a million men, including frontier guards. In addition, there is a wide network of volunteer assistants to the police, particularly in the rural areas. The two police ministries are the MVD, which is mainly concerned with large-scale control, day-to-day policing and the maintenance of the armed frontier, and the KGB (Committee for State Security), which controls the more secret activities. The security police which has been described as "The Sword of the Revolution", defending it against its secret enemies, has the curious record of having itself been controlled by enemies of the people for over twenty years, from the early 'thirties. Its successive heads, Yagoda, Yezhov, Merkulov, Abakumov and Beria, were all shot. It is true that for a short period before Stalin's death it was headed by a man never himself labelled a traitor, S. D. Ignatiev; but even under him it remained an agency of the enemies of the people—since his "political blindness" made him the dupe of his criminal Deputy Minister, Ryumin, also shot.

The most important element in the security set-up is the "Section for Investigating Specially Important Cases". The three chiefs of this section between 1946 and 1953 were also shot with their superiors. Beria, who was in general control for most of the time between 1938 and 1953, is now officially described by Khrushchev as "an agent of foreign imperialism". This seems to show some lack of sense of proportion. A previous security minister, Yagoda, when accused at his public trial in 1938 of being an agent of the imperialists, said that he had willingly confessed to his other criminal activities, but it would be absurd for him to admit

73

this one, since if it were true the imperialists would have had no need of an intelligence service at all. One would think that the same applied to Beria. It seems highly unlikely that many people, even in the Soviet Union, believe this sort of charge. The fact that it is thought useful and necessary to level it throws some light on government attitudes.

There seems little need to rub in the terrorism which the police have shown themselves capable of exercising at one time or another over the people and over the party itself: it is more important to realize that in the present comparatively relaxed period this pressure is not what it was. It must be pointed out, however, that this is a decision of the Party leadership. There is nothing in principle, if that decision were changed, to prevent the police reverting to their old habits. The instrument remains intact. This is said, not by way of encouraging a sterile pessimism, but to prevent a healthy optimism from becoming unrealistic and excessive.

Meanwhile, if the offences to "socialist legality" formerly practised by the police are now kept within bounds, the sort of regulatory action which the police forces administer in the ordinary course of events is of interest. For example, a Soviet "internal passport" is only to be issued on the production of a birth certificate, military service draft certificates, a certificate of domicile and a work certificate. It bears details of social position and nationality as well as name, date of birth and a record of military service. Entries are made in it on registration with the militia, on engagement for or dismissal from work, on marriage and divorce and on entry into a frontier zone.

Under the present "Regulation Concerning Passports" all those over the age of 16 are obliged to possess internal passports if they:

(*a*) permanently live in towns, workers' settlements,

district centres and localities where tractor stations are situated,

(b) live in the communities of Moscow Province, within 100 kilometres of Leningrad or 50 kilometres of Kiev, or in zones adjacent to all Soviet borders, or

(c) work on construction projects, water or railway transport or State farms.

These passports fall into the following three categories:

(a) *Indefinite:* for those aged 55 or over, Heroes of the Soviet Union, invalids and pensioners;

(b) *Five-yearly:* for those between the ages of 16 and 55 and

(c) *Temporary:* for those who have lost their passports or those entering a region where the passport system is in force from a region where it is not.

For those who have to hold internal passports the formalities involved by any change of address are considerable. Any change of domicile for a period of over 24 hours entails the registration of the passport with the militia at the place of arrival through the house caretaker or the housing administration in the towns or through the representations of the local soviets in the countryside.

Similarly, absence from the normal place of residence for more than one and a half months, except for business trips, leave, medical treatment, and so on, involves "de-registration" with the local militia. Changes of address and death also entail "de-registration".

Those *without* internal passports (with the exception of servicemen, those in hospital, and seasonal harvest workers) are forbidden to live in areas where the passport system is enforced. This particularly affects those 30-odd million peasants who have not the right to an internal passport. The only concession made to them is that they are allowed to visit the towns within their local province for a period not exceeding five days. Even then they have to register such visits with the officials.

Lenin vigorously attacked the then internal passport system in 1903. He said then:

"Passports must be abolished in Russia too (in foreign countries passports were abolished long ago) . . . no police officer . . . must be allowed to stop any peasant from settling down or working wherever he pleases. The Russian peasant is still the serf of the officials to such an extent that he is not free to move to a town or free to settle in a new district. . . . The governor knows better than the peasant what is good for the peasant. The peasant is a child who dares not move without authority. Is this not serfdom, I ask you?" (V. I. Lenin, "To the Rural Poor", 1903, *Selected Works*, Vol. II, p. 280).

The great element of Stalin's compulsion which the world knows was the Forced Labour Camp. In these enormous numbers of people were confined in conditions ranging from rigorous to murderous. In his Secret Speech Khrushchev says, in passing, that they were places where people "perished". The numbers involved have been variously estimated and in any case were not constant, but several approaches give, taking the most conservative estimate on each doubtful point, figures of not less than three million souls, almost throughout the Stalin period. One method is based on the NKVD's share in production as given in the confidential version of the State Plan for 1941. This enables a reasonable, if rough, estimate to be made of the labour force under police control. Another is the collection of reports of prisoners who, knowing the numbers in their own camp and the number of camps forming a given administrative group, can put these together to provide a rough total for a given area. There are also a few more or less direct figures from Soviet sources, though not in later years. In 1931 the number of newspapers sent to all places of detention in the Russian, Ukrainian and Byelorussian Republics was just over 365,000, and it is added that there was one newspaper for five inmates. The total in the three republics alone was then therefore over 1,850,000 (A. Vyshinsky, *From Prisons to Educational Institutes*, Moscow, 1934). This was at a time when the camps were just getting into their stride. It is interesting that the highest number of prisoners in Tsarist times, according to Soviet figures, was 183,000. Of these 33,000 were engaged in penal labour and 5,000 were politicals.

This is not the place to elaborate on the system. There are many first-hand accounts by reputable witnesses which can be referred to. The point is that for many years the threat of transfer to these horrible places, thousands of miles from home, hung over every Soviet citizen; and that the number of human beings despatched to a life of misery, toil and want was unprecedented.

To forget all this would be foolish and indeed contemptible: but it is equally important to realize that there have been major changes in Soviet penal policy, particularly in the application of forced labour penalties. Reforms have been made, or promised, in the administration of the camps —now renamed "colonies". As a result of three amnesties the number of forced labourers has been drastically reduced. According to a statement made by the Soviet Deputy Procurator-General, P. I. Kudryavtsev, to Professor Berman of Harvard University in May, 1957, as many as 70 per cent of prisoners had been released since March, 1953. There cannot have been less than about $2\frac{1}{2}$-3 million prisoners in Stalin's last years, so that there should now be at least three-quarters of a million.

Little of the unpleasantness of the Stalin method of rule was publicly codified at the time. But one item—now, again, happily eliminated—may serve to show the spirit of the period. Article 58 of the Criminal Codex was that which dealt with State crimes. One of its most striking provisions was 58.I.c. which provided for the punishment even of relatives who knew nothing of the crime, in the case of desertion abroad.

A Soviet law book justifies "the application of special measures in respect of the adult members of the family of a serviceman-traitor in the event of the latter's flight or escape across the frontier in those cases where the adult member of the family in no way contributed to the acts of treachery that was being prepared or executed and did not even know of it. ... The political significance of it consists in the strengthening of the overall preventive action of the criminal law for the purpose of averting so heinous a felony as the action of a serviceman in crossing or flying across the frontier, as the result of which the guilty party cannot himself be subjected to punishment. Those persons indicated . . . are liable to deprivation of electoral rights and to banishment to remote areas of Siberia for a period of five years" (A. A. Piontkovsky and V. D. Menshagin, *Course of Soviet Criminal Law*). This book came out two years after Stalin's death, when the law was still in force. It was superseded in 1958.

In September, 1953, a decree was issued abolishing the notorious MVD Court of Summary Procedure, which had been established in 1934. This was the body that had powers to sentence to forced labour and exile, officially up to five years, but in practice to unlimited sentences. The accused was given no opportunity to attend his trial, which was usually based on written evidence or instructions.

The new Criminal Law was published in December 1958. Excesses of the previous law have been removed, even if, in general, the improvements are mainly restorations of rights which have existed in theory all along. For instance, it is laid down that justice can be administered only by courts. This was constitutionally the position throughout the Stalin period, and had no effect on widespread trials by MVD *troikas*. Public trial is now guaranteed except in circumstances where the State rules otherwise for reasons of secrecy. The snag here is that a number of trials said to have been public—such as Abakumov's in Leningrad in 1954—can have been so only in some very technical sense. They were not announced and as far as is known no ordinary member of the public ever got into them. The judges are to be removable only by their electors and can be prosecuted only by decision of the Supreme Soviet. But these are conditions which can be fulfilled on a Party decision without difficulty. Apart from that, unfortunately, many of the rigours of the old laws still remain. For instance, ten years' imprisonment is the punishment for "propaganda with a view to undermining or weakening Soviet power . . . or spreading slanderous fabrications vilifying the Soviet state and socialist system, and likewise disseminating, preparing or keeping for this purpose literature of similar content".

The code, therefore, remains a draconic one, but its application is less disfigured by gross inhumanity than in Stalin's time. The fact that improvement has taken place may be interpreted in one of two ways: as a sign either of better intentions, or of the intention to preserve appearances better. Even the latter is at least something. But as in the Soviet past, the present law could perfectly well be administered in a terrorist fashion, and all the guarantees depend upon the goodwill of the Party.

One of the great distinctions between the attitude of the Soviet government to its citizens and that which applies in most of the outside world is the extreme difficulty a Russian finds in obtaining permission for unsponsored travel abroad, and particularly outside the Soviet bloc. This is a restriction which is very much resented by the ordinary intelligent Russian. It is universally reported by British and other visitors to the USSR that this is the one point which even keen supporters of the régime with whom they argue cannot find any method of justifying.

Life is certainly much better in the Soviet Union now than it was in Stalin's time. Personal security has gradually improved, and the standard of living has also gone up continually. Although there is a good deal still in the USSR which may strike the rest of us as deplorable, yet if improvement could be relied on to continue we might perhaps treat these as temporary phenomena on their way out. We cannot yet safely do so, however. In a number of respects things are already more difficult than they were in 1956, for example, and the present Party leadership has made it clear that there are definite limits to the increase in personal liberties which they are prepared to countenance. Yet while there cannot be any real guarantee that things might not get worse again, on balance, a very definite improvement must be noted since Stalin's death.

CHAPTER VI

PRESS, RADIO AND BOOKS

THE NATURE OF THE Soviet Press, and of the information reaching the Soviet peoples through the various official sources which are its exclusive purveyors, is a large study. But a few examples should give a clear enough impression for all practical purposes.

The general principles of Soviet Press work are often stated, and always in such terms as these:

"The Communist Party keeps a close watch on the ideological purity, the Marxist-Leninist strictness of our newspapers, periodicals and publications, discovering in good time and resolutely correcting any deviations from the Party's line" (*Novy Mir*, September, 1954).

How this affects the presentation of news is described by the chief of the Soviet news agency TASS:

"Information must not simply illuminate this or that fact or event, though there might be reason for such illumination; it must *also pursue a definite end*. Information must serve and help the solution of the fundamental tasks which face our Soviet society and our Soviet people as they proceed along the road of gradual transition from Socialism to Communism. Facts and occurrences must be selected for objects of information which serve and assist the solution by the Soviet people of the tasks confronting them in the building of Communism. *Information must be didactic and instructive*" (N. G. Palgunov, *The Fundamentals of Press Information: Tass and Its Role*, Moscow, 1955. His italics).

An idea of *Pravda's* news coverage is best gained by quoting the contents of a random issue in full. Here, for example, is the issue for June 5, 1958:

Front Page

2 column editorial: "Defence of Peace—The Sacred Duty of the Peoples".

1 column: Story of miner who achieved an economy of 1 rouble per ton of coal produced.

1½ columns plus picture: Arrival in the USSR of the King and Queen of Nepal.

2 columns: Letter from Khrushchev to supporters of nuclear disarmament movement.

1½ columns: Congress of the Bulgarian Communist Party.

Page Two

1 column: "The 40th Anniversary of the Formation of the Communist Party of the Ukraine".

½ column: "Plenum of the Tambov Province Party Committee".

30 lines: Courses for heads of branches of the Department of Agitation and Propaganda.

Short item: Half-yearly oil production plan fulfilled.

1 column: "A Week of Peace"—reports from various towns.

1½ columns: Report on agriculture by a Party Secretary.

Page Three

½ column: Favourable reactions by China, Poland and East Germany to Khrushchev's speech in Bulgaria.

½ column: News in brief (Albanian election results, trade agreement with Albania, proposed visit of delegation from Bonn to USSR, success of government troops in Indonesia)

¾ column: Departure of King and Queen of Nepal for USSR.

¼ column: Nehru's Press Conference.

Remainder of page: (about one-third): "It is essential to Fight to the Finish Against Revisionism"—quoted from Peking Daily.

Page Four

½ column: A hostile account of General de Gaulle's visit to Algeria.

1 column: Report of a Communist Front organisation meeting in Vienna.

¼ column: The situation in the Lebanon.

20 lines: Network of American rocket bases in Germany.

30 lines: Quotation from American article on launching of Sputnik.

10 lines: German industrialists visit Moscow.

3 news briefs: A conference, a festival, a visit by a minor statesman.

¼ column: Factory workers' visit to a tourist camp (with picture).

20 lines: Building a new road.

20 lines: Moscow theatre criticism.

5 lines: Exhibition of computing machines.

8 lines: Football match.

10 lines: Athletes depart for Belgrade.

30 lines: Admission of students to Party Schools.

Theatre programmes for the day.

Apart from the question of the objectivity or otherwise of the articles, and the absence of any competition, *Pravda* may be as strongly criticized for dullness and jejunity as some of our own newspapers are for sensationalism or worse. But it is positively thrilling compared with the output of the network of provincial papers in which lower grade journalists turn out the same sort of thing. As the Party's theoretical organ said, frankly, they are "stereotyped, hackneyed and

83

dry". It added "Let us take for example leading articles on the question of agriculture. Editorial staffs have a standard approach to this theme. As a rule they mention first the importance of the particular agricultural work which is imminent. Next are enumerated the names of the best collective farms and districts. Then follows the invariable 'however': 'However, by no means everywhere is real concern being shown . . .' and a number of negative examples are quoted. Then follows the conclusion: 'Such a situation is intolerable.' Finally the directive is laid down: 'Party and State organisations must . . .' and 'leaders of collective farms are obliged . . .' " (*Kommunist*, June, 1955).

Crime, accident, vice and so on, which occupy so much space in our mass-circulation newspapers, are not reported in the Soviet press except when it is considered necessary or suitable to do so on Party grounds. Recently a good many crimes of violence have been mentioned, especially in the papers of the Asian Republics, as part of a campaign against professional gunmen. A few months ago a Central Asian paper reported a striking gunfight on the roof of the Tashkent-Moscow Express—but this never made the Moscow papers. On the other hand, as an example of daring ingenuity given in the Moscow press, I remember a few years ago, during an earlier anti-crime campaign, a report of a gang who had stolen two Moscow fire engines and sold them to a collective farm.

"Speculation"—that is private trade—is constantly being attacked, but the amount of reporting on it depends on the pressure the Party is setting against it. Drunkenness is at present a suitable subject for exposure in the Press and so we get a number of tales of considerable human interest in that sphere.

A serious defect of the Soviet press is the absence of the more legitimate sort of "news". In December, 1957, a major earthquake occurred in Outer Mongolia. Peking Radio in December broadcast a brief report, mentioning that according to "preliminary estimated" 20 people were killed and 13 missing. The first mention of the disaster in the Soviet Press came towards the end of January, 1958, in a report published by Soviet scientists in *Izvestiya*. No mention was made of casualties. Again, on April, 1958, the Party daily newspaper in Turkmenistan published an article by the Minister of Internal Affairs of the Republic, devoted to the 40th anniversary of the Soviet Fire Service. This referred to a fire in an oilfield during 1957 which had lasted for 12 days before being put out. Twenty-eight members of the fire-fighting staff had been awarded certificates for bravery. This fire had never been previously mentioned.

Coal mining is a risky occupation, and, despite stringent safety precuations, accidents take place occasionally in every part of the world. Such accidents inside the Soviet Union, however, are almost never mentioned in print. Reports from German and Italian prisoners-of-war who have returned from the USSR, tell, for example, of a mining calamity which took place in Shakhty, in the Donets basin, during 1952. This was caused by an explosion which had destroyed ventilators. Dead and injured were believed to number over 1,000. It was never reported.

As to radio, it exhibits striking contrasts as between the narrowly political and the broadly cultural. On February 27, 1957, *all* the eleven items of news on the All-Union Radio consisted of meetings and conferences in Moscow, Leningrad, Kiev and Frunze (*Soviet Press*, No. 4, 1957). But here are a more typical day's programmes from Moscow Radio's Home Services (May 29th, 1958), and remarkable they are, if perhaps over-weighted on the side of officially approved music:

First Programme

9.30—Reading, "Pages of Reminiscences".

10.00—Rumanian play.

11.00—Book review.

12.20—Excerpts from Operettas.

13.15—Servicemen's requests.

14.05—Concert by young artists.

16.05—Talk on agriculture.

16.30—Peking speaking.

17.05—Amateur concert.

17.30—"What do You Know about Modern Production Methods?"

19.30—Modern Russian songs and dances.

20.00—Play.

23.00—Operatic arias.

Second Programme

10.30—Play.

12.00—Music of Dagestan.

13.15—Experiments in raising coal production—by a miner.

14.45—Piano recital.

15.20—Armenian State Choir.

16.00—Opera: *The Station-Master.*

17.15—Play.

18.40—For young listeners: "One of your Contemporaries".

20.00—Concert.

23.05—Chamber music.

Third Programme

19.20—Chamber music.

21.00—Works by Bashkir composers.

21.30—Recital by Pishchaev.

22.30—Recital by Dulova.

One of the most questionable features of Soviet radio is the vast and expensive jamming system which for years has prevented people listening to foreign stations. Khrushchev himself answered criticism of this in his interview with the Columbia Broadcasting Corporation on May 28, 1957:

"If the voice is good, we do not jam it. But if the voice jars on the ear, one tries to switch off the radio if possible, or if not, to jam this noxious voice."

A revealing, as well as self-contradictory, statement.

A good deal that has not been revealed about Soviet affairs may, as we have seen, be deduced by analogy from things that have been made public in Poland about parallel situations. In this case we can judge the extent and expense of the Soviet jamming operations from the far smaller Polish efforts. It was officially announced on November 24, 1956, that the Polish Government had stopped the jamming of foreign broadcasts. On January 24, 1957, it was stated that the yearly cost had averaged some 30 million zloty (£2·7 million) with an original capital outlay of 112 million zloty (£10 million).

It is striking enough that an effort of this sort can be put into plugging a minor ideological chink—for in ordinary circumstances what population is likely to be influenced much by a foreign radio's distant voice, competing with the vast and accessible apparatus of home publicity? It seems to show not simply distrust, but the most extreme distrust, of the Russian people's "reliability", as well as to make nonsense of the appeal to "peaceful competition" in ideas.

On the other hand the system has been relaxed on occasions, especially when the Soviet Government is seeking international détente, on the appearance of it. In 1956 the BBC was briefly exempted; and in 1959 the impending Summit brought a considerable measure of relief.

The Soviet Press and other publications are subject to a strict censorship. Its method of operation seems to have been altered lately, in the case of newspapers, more responsibility having been put on the editorial boards. The sign of censorship is the censor's number—a Cyrillic letter followed by five figures, usually at the bottom of the back page.

Before any book can finally appear in print for public consumption, it must undergo the following lengthy and complicated process, according to the laws governing *Glavlit*, the official censorship organ of the USSR. There are two stages of control—"Preliminary" and "Subsequent".

Before a printing house can accept an order to print, the manuscript must be accompanied by the permission of the local censorship organ. The printing house must then enter details of the order, and details of all subsequent stages in the process up to final publication, in a book which must be registered with the local police.

The order is now set up in type in strict conformity with the censored original. A first-proof is run off and submitted to the publishing house. The editor and the *Glavlit* representative write in all necessary "corrections", and the proof is returned to the printer stamped and signed.

The printer now makes the necessary typographical changes, runs off another copy and submits this once more to the publishing house. This is now inspected and signed by the editor, and the *Glavlit* representative signs, dates and stamps it on each sheet as "licensed for printing", together with the number of the licensing certificate. This completes "Preliminary Control". The licence to print is valid for three months only. A new licence must be obtained if it is desired to make any changes or if the work is transferred to another printer.

So far we have been covering "Preliminary control". "Subsequent control" goes as follows:

The printer may now run off 28 "pilot copies", and this number must not be exceeded. Pilot copies are immediately despatched for examination and final censorship to

(*a*) The Plenipotentiary of the Council of Ministers of the USSR for the Safeguarding of Military Secrets in Printed Materials;

(*b*) The Director of *Glavlit* of the RSFSR.

(*c*) The Publishing Sector of the Administration of Propaganda and Agitation of the Central Committee of the Party ("Agitprop");

(*d*) The MVD;

(*e*) The Ministry of Defence.

Agitprop receives 4 additional and the MVD 3 additional pilot copies of all "artistic, socio-political, children's and instructional literature".

Three pilot copies must also be sent to the publishing house which originally placed the order, and one copy, stamped "This corresponds with the copy licensed for printing", to the *Glavlit* censor, or the plenipotentiary of *Glavlit* attached to the publishing house who licensed the work for printing.

The publishing house now returns one pilot copy with a certificate signed by the responsible editor or the director giving the printer permission to run off the edition. In accordance with detailed regulations the first copies of the edition must be despatched as "obligatory copies" to the MVD and the Central State Book Chamber of the RSFSR.

Release to the public, however, is not authorized until

permission is given by the local representatives of *Glavlit*. Such authorization can be obtained only when the printing house has produced:

(*a*) The proof copy that was signed by the local representative of *Glavlit* for printing;

(*b*) The card bearing the necessary stamps confirming the despatch of the pilot and obligatory copies;

(*c*) One copy of the finished printed work with the publishing house's stamp, "This has been read for release to the public", with the responsible editor's signature.

The censor retains a copy and marks the other "Release to the public is permitted" and sends it back to the printer. Until permission is received no copies other than the pilot copies can be issued to the publisher. When permission is received binding and distribution can begin.

Cessation of printing may be ordered at any moment during this tedious process by *Glavlit* or its organs by telephone, telegraph or letter. When this happens all printing must be automatically stopped, finished books or sheets placed in carefully locked rooms pending special instructions, and not a single copy issued except to *Glavlit* functionaries. On receipt of written instructions to confiscate an edition, the entire finished production is sealed by a *Glavlit* representative. Removal and destruction of the edition is arranged by *Glavlit*.

When finally released, every printed work must carry, *inter alia*, the following information:

(*a*) Date of licence to print (expressed as: "signed for the press" with date);

(*b*) The number given to the order by the publishing house.

(c) The number of the local organ of *Glavlit* or its plenipotentiary.

That the provisions of this decree are still in force can be seen by inspection of the final page or the page immediately following the title page in most books, pamphlets or journals published in the USSR. Only publications in foreign languages and a few periodicals in Russian show no signs of having been censored. These exceptions include *New Times, Slavs*, and the *Journal of the Moscow Patriarchate*.

There are prospects of some streamlining of all this business. But there seems no sign of any change in the essentials of control. The account given does not cover what happens when one of the authorities *does* intervene. But Agitprop, for instance, has often done this lately, and a series of meetings has ensued in which Suslov and Pospelov, as Secretaries of the Party in charge of ideology, have become involved, and publishers and editors have been removed, and books suppressed. The process may take months.

Censorship is maintained on despatches going out from the Soviet Union, and Western correspondents frequently complain of the ham-handed fashion with which the censors handle their despatches. Khrushchev, however, claims that this is not censorship at all. His view, as expressed to Turner Catledge, of the *New York Times*, on May 10, 1957, is as follows:

"When this or that correspondent wishes to send abroad distorted reports which do not conform to the real state of affairs, our institutions take measures not to allow these incorrect, slanderous reports to appear. I hold this procedure to be correct. This, in effect, is not censorship but only a more rational use of material resources possessed by society, so as not to squander money on telegraphic communications, paper, etc."

At that time outgoing censorship in Moscow was becoming more severe. Just after General de Gaulle came to power in France, an American correspondent in Moscow sent a despatch which consisted solely of a quotation from the entry about de Gaulle in the *Large Soviet Encyclopaedia*. It was stopped altogether.

We may gain a particularly clear idea of the sort of information which is offered, and exclusively offered, to the Soviet people, if we look at some of the things that are taught about our own countries. Here we have experience against which we can judge what is said.

It must be emphasized at the outset that descriptions of life in the West have improved since Stalin's time, like everything else in the USSR. We no longer read of machine-guns being used against the workers of Camden Town and nothing lately has compared with such passages as the following from *Komsomolskaya Pravda* of 1st June, 1952:

"For us it is hard to imagine these dreary workers' quarters in London, Paris and New York, with their pitiful slums and stuffy workshops, where seven- and eight-year-olds toil all day and night, their faces emaciated and waxen."

Nevertheless, a few recent descriptions from among hundreds in responsible books or journals about British political life will serve to show what the Russian citizen and student is still led to believe:

"The Labour leaders secured power because the British workers believe their pre-election promises (the nationalization of the Bank of England and certain branches of industry, the improvement of the material position of the workers, the establishment of friendly ties with the Soviet Union). Having secured a majority of the seats in the House of Commons and having formed a government, the Right Labour leaders, however, began to carry out a policy very different from the one they had promised the electors" (B. S. Krylov, *The State Structure of Great Britain*, Moscow, 1957).

Whatever may be thought about that, it is hard to excuse such a downright falsehood as the following:

"Defenders of bourgeois democracy are lying when they say that the ballot in Britain is secret. Actually there is no secrecy." (A. Ioirysh and S. Shugaev, *Elections in Bourgeois Countries*, Moscow, 1957).

An account of the Labour Party's attitude to the independence of India runs in part:

"When at last the peoples of India as the result of a mighty upsurge of the national liberation movement were finally successful in securing political independence this happened in spite of the original intentions of Attlee's government and not because of them" (A. Rothstein, "British Reformism and the Colonial Problem", *Soviet Oriental Studies*, No. 6, 1957).

Few Britons would feel that the following, all that was said, was a full and objective account of British Communist policy in 1940:

"After France had been betrayed by its rulers and German aircraft began to scatter death in the thickly populated areas of Southern England, the communists demanded from the government the adoption of the most decisive measures against enemy air raids and collaboration with the anti-fascist movement of all the European peoples" (*Kommunist*, April, 1958).

As to the presentation of America, it is perhaps not surprising to read such explanations of why American workers have cars as the following:

93

"Take cars for instance. They are the most popular item sold on credit in the USA. This is to be explained by the fact that fares on the railways or buses in the USA are high. In addition, in many cases, town and suburban transport schedules are organized unsatisfactorily and a car is the only form of transport by which a worker can reach his place of work" (*Aid to Political Self-education*, June, 1958).

Some of the Soviet comment about foreign Socialist Parties are curious examples of that ability of some Russian commentators to make remarks which would seem to apply at least as strongly to themselves as to those they criticize, without this point apparently entering their heads. For instance, in a recent article on the Swedish Social Democratic Party they write: "The fact that the Party has for a long time headed the government has given it a great attractive force for all kinds of careerists" (*Questions of History*, June, 1958).

During the 1956 "Thaw" the Soviet periodical *Sovetskaya Muzika* (No. 7 of 1956) published a protest by a young Soviet composer against the supression by the directors of the Moscow Musical Conservatoire of a song by Robert Burns. The directors are accused of having excluded from a concert a song with words by Burns because it expressed Burns' preference for the "wind which blew from the West". Presumably this was a translation of Burns' "Of a' the Airts the Wind can Blaw" which begins:

> "Of a' the airts the wind can blaw,
> I dearly like the West,
> For there the bonnie lassie lives,
> The lassie I lo'e the best."

That is how the mind of a cultural bureaucrat works: and it is pleasant to observe that a Soviet periodical should have poked fun at such a ridiculous excess.

A false picture of the West is inculcated from early childhood. The following exercise sentences from school English textbooks give a representative selection of half-truths, total untruths and misleading destortions:

"Bourgeois governments always break the treaties they sign sooner or later."

"The work of making the banks of a river higher is the work of the Central Government. But the Central Government of the United States has no money for such work. It spends nearly all its money on preparations for a new war."

"The health of the children of English workers is never good."

"When a wage-earner in the United States dies or is disabled, the family loses the breadwinner and must starve."

"Most novels of modern bourgeois authors are worthless."

"In capitalist countries science serves the monopolists and not the people."

"According to the Wall Street imperialists, American children must be taught that banditry is a normal thing and that modern techniques will help to rob, kill and commit crimes. . . ."

The (Middle School) *Atlas of the History of the USSR* has an extensive series of maps on the Second World War. The key to the map for the whole period up to Stalingrad deals with the contributions of the Western Allies solely under the heading: "Breaches by the Anglo-Americans of their obligations as Allies." There are two sub-heads, viz.: "advances of the Anglo-American armies in second-rate and unimportant theatres of war"; and "Berne—place of secret negotiations between representatives of the USA and Fascist Germany".

It is difficult enough at the best of times for a people to form realistic and sound ideas of foreign countries. In the circumstances it is not surprising that staggering delusions about us are endemic in Russia. We have every right to object to this, if only in the interests of world peace.

CHAPTER VII

THE MIND OF THE SOVIET LEADERS
AND OURSELVES

WHAT TRULY MAKES Russia different from the countries of the West is that the Party feels empowered to organize every single sphere of the people's life. This does not mean, of course, that the average Soviet citizen is a cowering slave. The Soviet man or woman—or child—"in the street" lives, loves and dies, for the most part, in much the same way as his or her counterpart anywhere. What it does mean, however, is that the conditions for freedom of choice in intellectual, artistic, spiritual and even economic matters are, to the extent to which the Party exercises its power, totally absent.

This is not an invariable accompaniment of one-party rule, nor even of Communist rule. In Yugoslavia and Poland there are now many spheres in which the Party does not find an ideological war to fight. Even rock-and-roll, regarded in most of the Soviet bloc as a particularly deplorable manifestation of bourgeois culture, hostile to the Party's conception of life, has been "de-politicized" in Warsaw without results deleterious to the régime. We must hope for a similar development in the Soviet Union, but the signs of it, so far, are very few.

Surkov, the head of the Soviet Union of Writers, told Italian journalists (while he was in Italy attempting to secure the suppression of *Dr. Zhivago*) that it was better for a writer to be dictated to by an "intelligent Party" than by a stupid publisher. There is a whole Chinese box of fallacies in this statement. But leaving aside such obvious points as

96

the existence of more than one publisher and even the possibility that one might find an intelligent one, it is an extraordinary assumption that a political organization could ever be described as "intelligent" in the sphere of art. Even Lenin, when saying that he did not like Mayakovsky's poetry, could add that this was a field in which his competence was nil.

It is true that the Communist Party has admitted cultural mistakes committed over a long period of time. But the Central Committee is still held to be the respository of all wisdom, even in artistic matters. And the more one reflects on how the political leadership is selected, from men whose careers have been based on administration and ambition, on a fulltime fight for position and study of political issues and theories, the odder it appears.

This difficulty has been indirectly recognized by the Central Committee decree on music of May 28, 1958, which said that Muradeli's opera *The Great Friendship* had been wrongly condemned on the basis of the "subjective attitude of J. V. Stalin" who was "very negatively influenced by Molotov, Malenkov and Beria". But how can there be a non-subjective view on music, in the absence of absolutely clear objective criteria? A "Party" view can only be the consolidated "personal" view of the majority of a dozen, or a hundred, politicians.

Intervention in science follows the same pattern. Four pseudo-sciences, as the overwhelming majority of non-Communist specialists think them, have at one time or another become attached to Communist theory: Zhdanov aesthetics, Marr linguistics (now abandoned), Morgan anthropology and Michurin biology. The last, now represented by Lysenko, has caused the most trouble in the field of true science, ever since Vavilov, Russia's greatest biologist, perished in an Arctic camp as the result of opposing it. At

97

the time a prominent Soviet biologist who had opposed Lysenko's views (A. R. Zhebrak, himself a member of the Communist Party) had to make the following formulation in *Pravda* of August 15, 1948:

"So long as our Party recognized both tendencies in Soviet genetics, and disputes between those tendencies were reviewed as creative debates of theoretical questions in contemporary science, thereby assisting in the discovery of the truth, I steadfastly defended my views which in part differed from the views of Academician Lysenko. Now that it has become clear to me that the basic postulates of the Michurin school in Soviet genetics have been approved by the Central Committee of the Communist Party, I, as a member of the Party, do not consider it possible for me to retain a position that has been recognized as erroneous by the Central Committee. . . ."

The nature of Communist discipline in intellectual matters has never been more clearly expressed.

The geneticists of the Soviet Union were removed from their posts and some of them were imprisoned. Lysenko, in an article published shortly after Stalin's death, maintained that Stalin himself had collaborated with him in his major theoretical statement and even drafted part of it.

In post-Stalin times Lysenko's reputation fluctuated. He was criticized in 1954 and in the following years the suppressed voices of his opponents, the practitioners of Soviet genetic science, were again permitted. The magazine which had been particularly attacked in Stalin's time, the *Botanical Journal*, resumed its criticisms of Lysenkoism. But Khrushchev said in 1957 that he was personally in favour of Lysenko, and in December, 1958, Lysenko, though technically not even a Party member, had the extraordinary honour of being asked to address a meeting of the Central Committee. Khrushchev took the occasion to attack *The Botanical Journal* for criticizing him, and shortly afterwards its Editorial Board was purged. In June, 1956 he further attacked the genuine geneticists, and publicly demanded the removal of one stubborn one even from the provincial post to which he had been relegated. He added that "life itself" had proved the Lysenkoites right—for they had received Lenin prizes!

The horrifying thing about this is that there are evidently powerful forces within the Party which are still prepared to impose their own judgement, in scientific matters, even against the clear opinion of most of the experts. The hopeful thing is that, directly an opportunity was given, the voice of these experts could still be heard: though the second suppression, coming after an interim period of toleration, says little for the good sense of the Khrushchevist mind.

The idea that a party decision is superior to a factual demonstration is a form of withdrawal from the real world into an imaginary universe constructed according to theoretical specifications, but unfortunately ones which do not happen to apply to actuality. Not only that, obsession with the idea that everything is part of a political pattern leads to a way of speaking that one is almost tempted to call paranoid. Two of the commonest phrases in Soviet speeches are "*ne sluchayno*"—"it is not accidental", used to assert a connection between two events when no evidence (and often no likelihood) of such a connection exists; and "*kak izvestno*"—"as is known", used in lieu of proof to give weight to a highly controversial assertion. These are only the superficial signs of a basic method in which certainty replaces reason and proof.

The greatest difficulty of conducting rational discourse with the Soviet leadership, whether as between statesmen on the issues of peace and war or on abstract questions of literature or history, lies here. They take the view that no opinion other than the Party view of the moment is reputably motivated, carrying to an extreme a tendency characteristic

99

of politicians everywhere. Non-Communist opinions are automatically labelled the products of a desire, usually conscious, to preserve or restore an anti-Socialist form of society. But it goes further than this: any opinion held even by a veteran Communist or experienced Marxist which conflicts with the Party line is also "objectively" pro-capitalist. And so it is not possible, as British Labour leaders and American Trade Union chiefs both found in their discussions with Khrushchev in 1956 and 1959 respectively, to conduct discussions on matters of principle at all. The mind is closed, the arguments circular, and the reaction to non-agreement—abuse.

But how is the correct view defined? It is simply the majority opinion of the Party Congress, the Central Committee or the Presidium. For instance, after Lenin's death the Party wrongly, as is now admitted, ignored his advice to remove Stalin from the post of General Secretary. Again, in Stalin's time decisions now stated to be incorrect were taken. The decrees of December, 1956, and February, 1957, about the reorganization of industry are totally opposed to each other. The latter is now right, which leads to the presumption that the former was wrong.

The Soviet spokesmen think, or at least speak, in terms of grand abstractions—"the Party", "the working class"—as having made the correct decisions. But these general groupings do not have some collective supermind, any more than do the various nations which we ourselves are inclined to personalize. In practice decisions are taken by individual men, in however large numbers. Moreover, if it is clear that the Central Committee, and "the Party" itself, have been wrong on certain occasions, it is also obvious that a working class as such is not infallible by Soviet standards. The British working class, for example, has consistently shown itself to be well over 90 per cent. incorrect in its failure to vote for the candidates of the British Communist Party.

As for the Central Committee, there is no basis for any view that it is an automatic concentration of all that is best even in the Party. Stalin's victory over the opposition Communists in the late 'twenties was attributable much more to his ability as General Secretary to pack the congresses, than to the Party masses having any spontaneous nose for the right solution.

In any case, the notion that the Party has this metaphysical power, which need not be proved but simply asserted, to interpret Marxism correctly and to express the hidden thoughts of the working class, must be compared with the regularity with which the figures that have risen to the top have turned out to be traitors, tyrants or selfish power-addicts. It is not merely that almost all the leading figures of the Communist Party, as it existed when it came to power, were exposed in the 'thirties, but even most of the replacements who took the line still deemed correct about collectivization have fallen by the wayside, too. It is also true that the legitimacy of the Party descent of the present Central Committee seems disputable. As Khrushchev revealed in his Secret Speech, Stalin had a majority of members of the pro-Stalin 1934 committee and of the Congress which elected it shot without even the correct formalities, and packed these organs with his own nominees, so that the whole Party organization ever since traces back to the doubtfully legal cadres who obtained their position in 1937-8. Many of these, like Khrushchev himself, still hold power personally and almost all other posts of any significance at all are in the hands of their nominees.

At the absolute centre of the Soviet official view is the thesis that the government and the Communist Party "represent" the working class: and this claim did not receive total, unanswerable refutation until recently. After Stalin's death, and in particular in 1956, this came. Strikes, and risings led by the workers, took place in East Berlin and Pilsen in 1953. And in 1956 the greater events in Poland and Hungary exposed the whole fallacy.

The strikes and riots in Poznan in June, 1956 were admitted by the Polish leadership to have been caused by a complete loss of faith in the "Workers' Party" on the part of the working class. And in Budapest the workers not only formed the backbone of the rising, but carried on a bitter general strike long after the fighting had been put down, against the whole power of the occupation army and of the reorganized Communist state. The building workers of the Stalinallee in Berlin, the Zispo machinery workers at Poznan, the Csepel steel workers and the Tatabanya minders in Hungary quite simply destroyed the foundations of the Communist view. Not once but three times the entire working class was ranged against the Party machine and the "workers' state". In each case the working class had had years of experience of "its own rule" and had had access only to the Party's teachings and interpretations. Nor were these great strikes and risings easy undertakings. On the contrary, they were desperate affairs, setting the workers against the whole apparatus of the State, the armed police, and in the last resort the armies of occupation. It was shown that it was possible for the Marxist-Leninist Party to be regarded with bitter hostility by the class it was supposed to represent.

The only real way in which anyone can be known to represent any nation, class or any other group is by free election. To make any other claim—for instance to say, "I represent their real interests even if they don't like it"—is to arrogate to the "representer" the right of deciding for the group what is good for it: he then represents only his own opinions.

That the Russian leaders have involved themselves in contradiction on this sensitive point seems obvious. For twenty years elections have been taking place at which only one candidate has presented himself, but in which the ballot forms print an instruction to the voter to cross out the names of all but one of the candidates, according to choice. The very word "elect" means, in Russian as in English, the making of a choice. And the Soviet elections are, of course, frequently defended as "the freest in the world". The thought processes involved in accepting this position (and others on similar themes) are peculiar.

If the word "represent" is used to blur a good deal of awkward reality in the political field, in the social field the culprit is "own". All economic measures are justified on the grounds that the workers "own" the economy and therefore cannot have any interests conflicting with the Plan. But in what sense, other than the purely verbal and doctrinal, do the workers own the factories?

To quote Mr. Anthony Crosland, "either collectivism or private ownership is consistent with widely varying degrees of liberty, democracy, equality, exploitation, class feeling, planning workers' control and economic prosperity" (C. A. R. Crosland, *The Future of Socialism*). As Mr. Crosland argues, it is the degree to which these attributes are present or absent in a given country which makes people differentiate between societies, rather than the often formal criterion as to who is the "owner" of factories.

A Soviet on-the-spot comment shows some of the reality:

"We have kolkhozniks who are careless about common property. Once I reproached one of them for squandering the kolkhoz harvest, and I reminded him that he was a part owner of the common property. He grinned sarcastically and sneered:—

"Nice lot of owners! It is all empty talk. They just call us

owners to keep us quiet, but they fix everything themselves. . . ."

"A real kolkhoznik won't say, when he sees the chairman
drive past in his car, 'Here am I, part-owner of the kolkhoz,
tramping along on foot, while he takes his ease in a
"Pobeda". Any kolkhoznik who really cares for his kolkhoz
will agitate to see that the chairman should have his own
car! The kolkhoznik, like the Soviet worker, is interested in
strengthening the management of his economy' " (*Party
Life*, December, 1957).

As to "liberty", a typical Soviet argument may be briefly
developed. Let us take the question of the freedom of the
press. The normal Soviet view is that the Soviet press is
"free" since paper, presses, etc. are made available to "workers' organizations". Clearly the word "free" is not here used
in the sense in which it would normally be employed. But
if one urges the fact that only one opinion, or one version of
events, is tolerated, while in the West any number may be
expressed, the Soviet retort is that the Western Press belongs
to capitalists, and prints lies. It goes on to maintain that
anyone criticizing the Soviet set-up and preferring the
"freedom" allowed in Western countries is thereby proved
to be an enthusiastic supporter of lies and capitalism. But this
is naturally quite irrelevant. One can concede that it is a
bad thing in principle that newspapers should be owned by
irresponsible private persons in the West and one can be
strongly opposed to any abuses that ensue. And one may
allow the possibility that some form of free Press not depen-
dent on private ownership may be devised. Yet the fact
remains that, with all its faults and disadvantages—and they
are glaring—at present the press of the West is free, in Rosa
Luxemburg's sense, and that of the Soviet Union is not.

In fact, to criticize Soviet arrangements is not to eulogize
those of the West. To claim that our institutions are more

humane than those of the Soviet Union is not to justify "capitalism".

Whatever foreign policy we may decide to support, it will be agreed that it should at least not be based on a misunderstanding of Soviet reality. That the Soviet long-term aim is to secure Communist rule throughout the world is not in doubt. That they have no qualms in principle about the use of force, as in Hungary in 1956, is equally indisputable. It is true that they expect, or appear to expect, that capitalism will eventually wreck itself, so that only a limited amount of violence might be required to destroy it. The classic idea has been that the seizure of power in any country would be carried out by local Communist parties, and the Russians have frequently called foreign communists to their duty in terms like the following:

"The proletarian internationalist is he who in his love for his native land protects without any reservation the Soviet Union" (*Kommunist*, No. 11, 1959).

But in fact, in the case of the present Communist states of Eastern Europe, the Communist parties came to power after, and as a result of, the entry of Soviet troops. In our diplomatic protocol it may be necessary to go through the motions of treating the Hungarian Government as sovereign, but we can hardly be misled into thinking that it owes its existence to anything but the massive use of Soviet power, in November, 1956.

The desire to secure the world for one method of rule does not signify war in all circumstances. Otherwise medieval Europe would have been in a permanent state of crusade. There are good reasons for avoiding gullibility in the appraisal of Soviet intentions, but this does not in itself mean either that the Russians plan a world war, or that some sort of *modus vivendi* cannot be reached on a realistic basis: and it is so important that we should do everything we can to try to reach it that most of our other preoccupations must pale in comparison. If even the present uneasy truce can be maintained over a period, it is at least possible that changes may take place in the conditions now producing tension. In any case, clear and cool heads are required, and a determination not to be deluded by either our hopes or our fears.

Khrushchev has put forward as a basis for international relations the line of "peaceful competition". If we must accept the present Soviet view that two systems of ideas, power and economies stand irrevocably opposed to each other, then peaceful competition between them is clearly an admirable notion. But there is a real snag, and we must face it: if the competition is conducted under Soviet rules it entails that Soviet ideas may be propagated in the West, but not Western ideas in the Soviet Union, and that Communist Parties may compete in democratic elections, but democratic parties may not be allowed in Communist elections. This leaves things extremely one-sided, and rubs in the importance of seizing the present increased opportunities of "penetrating" the Soviet Union by visits from members of the general public, politicians, business men, scientists, professional men, and so on.

There is something else we must face, if we are to strive for peace with all the facts before us: in their thesis that the whole world must become "socialist" the Soviet leaders have always made it clear that by this they mean that all countries should come under the control of Communist Parties. Experience in countries where this has occurred shows that there is a very strong implication here of following the Soviet line whenever Moscow is in a position to enforce it. It is true that the Russians from time to time speak of other "roads to socialism". But even at their easiest, these have never amounted to more than minor tactical concessions. The Yugoslav way, for instance, is inadmissible.

At the 20th Soviet Party Congress, which marked the highest point of ideological concession, there were many general statements about different countries being allowed to have their own "road" to socialism, of the possibility of carrying out a revolution by parliamentary means and of co-operation with other Socialist parties. But even then they attacked "reformism". Mikoyan said: "the working class must indefatigably fight against reformism", and also: "cases are known where certain Socialist parties have gained a majority in their parliament. In some countries there have even existed and still exist Socialist governments. However, even then their activities are restricted merely to small concessions in favour of the workers; no socialism is built", and, again, "Reformists . . . in essence were and remain advocates of capitalism".

The assertion of "different ways to socialism" was also spoilt by the fact that it was pointed out by Suslov, for example, that "The historical experience of the origin and development of the socialist system in quite a number of countries has now fully confirmed Lenin's brilliant foresight that, whilst maintaining the unity of the main and most important matters and common paths, the transition to socialism in various countries will not be quite the same and that each nation will make its own contribution to one form of democracy or another, to one form of the dictatorship of the proletariat or another . . .". The different "ways to socialism" do therefore not imply any greater differences than exist between the countries of Eastern Europe (as was explicitly said by other speakers). And in no circumstances do they mean either that the Communist Party will not be in charge, or that the Soviet idea of "socialism" may be departed from.

As to the matter of attaining "socialism" by parliamentary means, it was stated by Suslov that in certain states "the possibility is not excluded of the working class coming to power peacefully, or of its gaining majority in parliament and turning parliament, in effect, into a people's parliament". However, he qualified this by saying that this could only work when "backed by a mass revolutionary movement". If this was the line at the period of maximum relaxation, it is not surprising that the views expressed at present are tougher and more uncompromising still. This is particularly so since the renewed assault on Tito and "revisionist" Communism which started in 1958.

The Soviet rulers in effect deny the legitimacy of all non-Communist régimes, and look to their eventual replacement by Soviet-type Communist ones. Meanwhile, however, they are perfectly prepared to deal with them on a pragmatic basis: and, however unwelcome their long-term ideas may be to the rest of us, we could do well, in the meantime, to be as pragmatic as they are. But we need to keep our eyes open.

CHAPTER VIII

WORKERS AND OTHERS

THE LIVING AND WORKING conditions of the people of the USSR have in the past varied, roughly speaking, with the amount of effort the government was putting into heavy industry: and the development of heavy industry has of course been, in a country like Russia, a crux (the question being to what extent the present generation ought to be sacrificed for the sake of future ones). In the forthcoming. period Khrushchev has committed himself to an increase in both heavy industry and consumer goods, even though the former is by far the more heavily financed. Meanwhile we may see how the worker actually lives.

The official stereotype of the Soviet employee is of a free worker, eagerly fulfilling his plan and being rewarded with good conditions. The hostile stereotype is of a sweated slave. But though individual factories vary considerably, and individual workers view things differently, nowhere is there much resemblance to either.

Lenin's declaration of April, 1917, that the pay of any official "must not exceed that of a competent workman", found expression in legislation immediately after the Revolution. But compromise began almost at once. By the autumn of 1918 salaries of specialists had been allowed to rise to more than double that even of the highest grade of workers. Under Stalin a definite policy of high rewards for officials and for particularly productive workers came in. The most important method of differentiating workers' wage scales has been the widespread use of piece-work systems. In 1955, "almost three-quarters" of the workers in industry were on piece-work, according to official figures. In 1955 it was stated "the progressive norm [The amount of piece-work required to earn the wage is called the norm: "progressive" means that it is continually raised] is an enormous organizing force for the broad masses in the struggle for the undeviating growth and perfection of Socialist production" (Chigvintsev, *Wages under Socialism*, Moscow, 1955).

There are signs of a turn towards time-rates in the most modern and automated factories employing highly skilled labour, and this trend will doubtless become more pronounced. But at present, and for a good time to come, the effect of the norm system and of greatly differential wage scales is to put very high pressure on the lowest grades and high enough pressure on most workers. The result desired is simply increased production. Pensions, too, are openly used for this purpose. ". . . This differentiation in pension rights is a weapon in the struggle for the creation of reliable qualified staff and the further increase in labour productivity" (G. N. Moskalenko, *State Social Insurance*, Moscow, 1953).

Mikoyan stated, in 1954, that the "average money wage of workers and employees in industry in 1953 reached 219 per cent of the 1940 level". As average yearly wages in 1940 amounted to 4,050 roubles, the figure for 1953 works out at about 8,150 roubles. Allowing for various subsequent official statements, wages in 1956 would have reached 8,400 roubles, or 700 roubles a month. In 1959 it was stated to be 785 a month.

There is a wide range about the mean. In workers' supply shops in the coal industry, 40,000 workers earned on average slightly less than 500 roubles in 1956, and on state farms and Machine Tractor Stations in Moscow Province the figure was approximately 400 and 500 roubles respectively.

Auxiliary building workers in Moscow received 550 roubles. In local government employment in Altai Territory earnings were 525 roubles. Skilled workers may receive 1,200 roubles and more. Salaries up to 20,000 roubles a month and even more may be found among senior Party and Government officials, Academicians, scientists, and so on. A typical salary for a factory director is 10,000 roubles, to which must be added bonuses and perks; the President of the Academy of Sciences is supposed to be paid 23,000 roubles a month, over 60 times the wage of an unskilled worker. The difference is great by any standard. And, even though the old financial egalitarianism of a Bernard Shaw appears to be dead in Socialist parties everywhere, including the British, the Russian *priviligentsia* benefits to an extent which most socialists would still find it hard to swallow.

We have seen something of the present food situation in Chapter V. The most useful calculation of the relative purchasing powers of currencies of various countries is based on the valuation in current prices of a given average consumption of goods and services. On this basis (and for personal consumption estimates only) a rouble equals between fourpence halfpenny and fivepence, and the Soviet workers' average earnings carry a purchasing power of about £3 8s. 0d.-£4 0s. 0d. per week at best.

According to the latest Ministry of Labour data, British industrial manual workers earnings average £10 14s. 0d. per week. (A comparison between all workers, town and country, would give a far greater lead to the British.)

The Soviet Seven-year Plan (1959-65) pledges an increase of "real incomes" of Soviet workers by 40 per cent. (Money incomes will rise as follows: the average from 785 roubles a month to 990, and the minimum from 350 to 600.) If all goes well the Soviet worker thus hopes to earn, seven years hence, something like a half of what his British colleague earns at present. The Soviet authorities are therefore unwise in inviting the comparison: for the British standard of living is far higher than that of some other countries which the Russians could cite with greater effect.

Of the Soviet Trade Unions all that really needs to be said is that as they are unable to pit themselves against the employer, most trade unions in other countries do not regard them as genuine but "yellow". The Soviet view is that the State, which is the employer, is a workers' State, so that it would be absurd for a workers' organization to oppose its decisions.

"Conducting all their work under the direction of the Communist Party . . . the trade unions consolidate the workers and employees around the Party, mobilize them for a fight for fresh victories in the building of Communism" (*Soviet Trade Unions*, February, 1956).

And again:

"Party committees are in duty bound skilfully to channel the work of trade union bodies, constantly to help them perform their functions" (Resolution of the Central Committee, December, 1957).

That these bodies are not as effective as they might be in protecting workers' rights is now not infrequently admitted. They are supposed to secure at least that the legal position is not infringed by the management—a fairly mild piece of protection. Yet *Leninskoye Znamya* of October 28, 1958, described a carpenter at a building materials combine who protested after being "forced to work 18 hours a day for two weeks", and was dismissed on the spot by the Director. Moreover, "the Labour Disputes Commission and the Trade Union works committee recognized the dismissal as just". The writer added the corollary: "Unfortunately, this is not an isolated case". This type of criticism is a useful safety-valve for the Soviet régime, and may offset, to a limited degree, what any Western Socialist must regard as the general ineffectiveness of the Soviet Trade Union system.

Trying to find the causes of these recurring defects of the system, the writer suggested that they were "born of the bureaucratism of certain directors of enterprises and institutions, of indifference, conceit, self-righteousness and lack of responsibility for work taken on. Such managers as these, who sometimes ignore the Soviet labour laws, unjustifiably dismiss or transfer a worker and do not pay on time or at the correct rates, also commit other breaches of the law." And, in spite of a decree of July 15, 1958, "Trade union organizations are still not energetic enough in fighting breaches of labour laws, and in many cases do not defend the legal claims of the workers. . . . Particularly widespread breaches of labour laws are failure to give workers their annual holidays at the correct time, unfounded transfer by the administration of rest-days without the agreement of the unions, and the illegal use of overtime." There were also "gross breaches" of legislation on working hours for adolescents between sixteen and eighteen.

"We are all suffering from spells of overtime", wrote a worker to *Party Life* in June, 1956. "We work overtime, lose our rest-day, expend unnecessary labour, time and nervous energy, and the men guilty of all this get a prize for fulfilling the programme." Another case in the same month, when late supplies had held up work, was described in a leading article in *Trud*:

"When the required parts eventually reach the works, the spurt begins, rest-days are cancelled and the workers have to labour 12 or 14 hours a day. It is useless to look for a record of overtime worked: it is not accounted for, and payment is arbitrary."

As for the complaint of bureaucracy, a recent report in a trade union magazine describes how "an ordinary fitter" in a factory at Chimkent had to have forms signed, initialled or filled in by 19 people, taking him eight days, between reporting for his new job and starting work (*Soviet Trade Unions*, June, 1958).

In 1953, 14,000 Labour Reserve School pupils had no jobs ready for them when they finished their training; and in 1955 more than 18,000 (*Kosomolskaya Pravda*, December 2, 1956). Managements have been ready to flout the law on hours on occasion; sometimes the young worker is worked the full adult working day (*Sovetskaya Kirgiziya*, March 22, 1957), sometimes his wages are reduced (*Molodoy Kommunist*, No. 11, 1956), but more often managements refuse to take on young people, to whom they have to pay the same wages for less work.

Cases of juvenile unemployment deriving from this cause are reported from towns all over Russia. The position of young people with secondary school education and ambitions to get into a Higher Educational Establishment is particularly parlous. One report quotes the typical attitude of a factory personnel department towards applications from such young people:

"There's a lot of fuss with you, and precious little to show for it. You have to be taught a trade; as adolescents you have to be let off two hours early from work; and then, as soon as you do get the hang of it, in a moment you're back in the Higher Education Establishment to take your exams! . . . No, that sort of manpower just isn't profitable for production. We're fulfilling a plan; we haven't the leisure to fuss over you . . ." (*Literaturnaya Gazeta*, November 20, 1956).

"We're fulfilling a plan"—that, combined with a measure of unimaginativeness, inefficiency and bureaucratic excess which are not exclusively Soviet or Russian, is the ultimate explanation of all such abuses. Two views are possible: one is that the plan is all-important, and that the abuses are relatively of less account; the other is that what matters most of all is the present situation of individuals, and particularly of young people. Whatever may be taught about this, however, the point is that, despite a good deal of "self-criticism" of the kind described, Soviet Trade Unions are far less effective in preventing such abuses than British ones: indeed their action in this respect is limited to vigilance against the State's breach of its own labour regulations.

In most families the women must also earn. In 1956, a delegation of the British National Union of Mineworkers visited Russia. In the pits they visited, the ratio of women was between 10 and 15 per cent of the whole labour force. The British delegates said that at one mine the women onsetters had to work eight hours in the wettest conditions they had ever seen, with water pouring down a new shaft and the men at the bottom looking more like lifeboat crews than miners.

The Soviet *Literary Gazette* of July 12, 1956, describing working conditions in the coalmines said: "At first it is hard, especially for girls. Valya Pchelnikova is only 20; in 1954, she finished 10 years school in Orel, lived about a year with her parents and was bored, not knowing what to do. Someone advised the girl to go to the Donbas and here she became keen on mining work. She started work at the Lutugin mine and became a shotfirer's assistant." *Kazakhstanskaya Pravda* wrote on March 7, 1954: "The Communist Party has opened the wide road to active labour for Kazakh women. Thousands are working in the coalmines of Karaganda." The same paper reported on January 8, 1955: "The number of women employed in the coal industry increased by 8,000 in 1954." There are now prospects that this type of heavy work for women will be gradually brought to an end.

At the 21st Party Congress in January, 1959, the forthcoming abolition of direct taxation was announced. Lenin wrote that direct taxation was the method most favourable to the poor, since it can be graded according to wealth, while taxes on cigarettes or food cannot. In the USSR direct taxation has hitherto not been so heavily weighted in favour of the lower income groups as in most countries, staying at a flat 13 per cent for all higher incomes.

The main sources of state revenue in the USSR have been indirect taxation, direct taxation and the compulsory state loan. The last was discontinued in 1959, and the second will shortly go too, leaving only the indirect or "turnover" tax. The proportion of the state revenue to come from the three sources in the 1957 budget was as follows (in thousand million roubles):

Turnover tax . . .	277
Direct taxes	52
Subscription to the State loan .	28
Total	357

Thus the turnover tax, whose exact rates on given commodities have never been published, is by far the greatest source of income.

In 1957 the Soviet wages lists (in the *Plan Fulfilment Report* for the year) show 52 million employed. The average pay was about 700 roubles a month, giving a total of 404 thousand million roubles a year. Pensions totalled 58 thousand million. The income of the peasantry is harder to assess: an estimate of sales in the free market gives about 40 thousand million. The dividends paid by the collective farms to members amount to about 45 thousand million. Peasants' income in kind is probably the equivalent of about 75 thousand million roubles. Thus, including income in kind, the total income of the population for 1957 was approximately 658 thousand million roubles, which can be compared with the taxation figure.

Housing has always been a weak spot in Soviet life, at least since Stalin came to power. "If one compares the figures on the size of the urban population with the figures of the Housing Fund, it transpires that in 1955 with regard to the supply of housing space to the population . . . we remain at the 1913 level and below the level for 1926. Compared with 1940, however, the supply of housing space had increased in 1955 by 6 per cent approximately" (*Kommunist*, June, 1956). The magazine mentions the 1955 living space as 7·3 square metres a head. It is lower in the cities of Central Asia—5·8 in Alma Ata, Frunze and Stalinabad, the local capitals. But according to the Soviet statistical handbook published in 1956 (*The National Economy of the USSR*) "living space", *excluding* kitchen, corridor and so on, averages less than five square metres (i.e. 53 square feet) per person.

It was stated in *Sovietskaya Rossiya* of June 18, 1957, in an article on the housing problem, that 46 million square meters of floor space were to be built during the year, so that "between five and six million people could move to new flats". That is to say, it was expected that the average space per person would be 8/9 square metres, *including* the kitchens which are at present usually communal in Soviet blocks of flats.

A Moscow home service broadcast of March 31, 1957, by a prominent architect, predicted a trend away from "communal flats" to "one-family flats". Although communal flats had at one time seemed the most economical solution, he said, the use of a communal kitchen, etc., was undoubtedly inconvenient. "There can be no doubt that the gradual transition to one-family flats will vastly improve the living conditions of the population." Delays and troubles are more widely reputed from the building industry than from any other. (There was recently a complaint that a new block of flats in Tashkent had waited seven years (so far) for a water supply.) Even after the total fulfilment of the present Plan, the average living space will be below the 9 square metres per person which is the Soviet official sanitary minimum.

In general, conditions of life for the poor in the USSR are hard, even very hard, by present British standards, and there is no doubt of the existence of a powerful desire to have them changed. It is undeniable, however, that a considerable improvement has taken place since the truly miserable forties, and there seems every prospect of their improving still further: it would be well for us, moreover, as a safeguard against self-righteousness, to recall the condition of the "depressed areas" in our own country between the two world wars. We seem to have beaten that bogy: and we must hope that the Russians will beat theirs.

CHAPTER IX

MINORITIES

IT MAY BE SAID, in general, that some of the least praiseworthy aspects of life in the Soviet Union are those least attacked, and some of the most praiseworthy are those most attacked. So it is in the matter of the minorities. We often hear that the Soviet Union has been exemplary in her dealing with these minorities. This is not so.

On a proper treatment of the subject, the whole question of nationalism—its desirability or otherwise, its virtues or its vices—ought to be thoroughly reviewed. Such a treatment is impossible here: all that can be done is to set down a few undoubted facts about the Soviet scene.

The minorities of Russia enjoy, on paper, exemplary minority rights, and have done so for a generation. Most of these peoples are a Soviet inheritance from Tsarist imperialism. Many have a hereditary hatred of Russia. We may consider the typical case of the Chechens, a nation of half a million in the North Caucasus. One of Tolstoy's stories, "Hadji Murad", describes Chechens returning from the mountains where they had taken refuge after a Russian raid on their village:

"No one spoke of hatred of the Russians. The feeling experienced by all the Chechens, from the youngest to the oldest, was stronger than hate. It was not hatred, for they did not regard those Russian dogs as human beings, but it was such repulsion, disgust, and perplexity at the senseless cruelty of these creatures, that the desire to exterminate rats, poisonous spiders, or wolves—was as natural an instinct as that of self-preservation."

When the Bolsheviks were seeking power they not only made use of the hatred of the Chechens and other oppressed nations of Russia for the Tsarist régime, but also worked out principles whereby national oppression was to end, and national hatreds were to be eliminated, by the granting of autonomy and equality. On the day after the seizure of power, November 8, 1917, the Soviet Government published a decree which ran in part:

"If any national whatsoever is retained as part of a given State by force, if, despite its expressed desire— whether expressed in the press, in popular assemblies, in the decisions of political parties, *or by rebellions and insurrections against national oppressions* [my italics] it has not the right of choosing freely (the troops of the annexing or, generally, the more powerful nation being completely withdrawn and without any pressure being brought to bear) the constitutional forms of its national existence, then its incorporation is an annexation, that is, seizure and coercion."

For the previous century the Chechens had carried on a bitter struggle against the Tsar's generals. From 1818 until 1859, the first edition of the *Large Soviet Encyclopedia* tells us, the Chechens were "the most active and strongest opponents of the Tsarist Government during the conquest of the Caucasus". They rebelled again in 1877 and in 1905.

During the Russian civil war they fought, under their Emir, Uzun Hadjii, against the White General Denikin. In 1922 the Chechen Autonomous Province was set up, and in 1936 they were formed into an "Autonomous Republic" with their smaller brother nation, the Ingushi. At the beginning of the Second World War the two peoples together numbered about 500,000.

All Soviet literature up to this time described the lot of the inhabitants of these distant valleys as a particularly happy one. *Izvestiya* (January 15, 1939) compares their experiences under the Tsars ("The history of Checheno-Ingushetia— decades of bloody struggle of a freedom-loving nation against the colonisers") with their present happy lot ("Under the sun of the Stalin Constitution has flowered luxuriantly the culture of the Chechen-Ingush people, national in form and socialist in content".) In August, 1942, a pamphlet published by the Soviet State Publishing House described them as "united by a common feeling of hatred towards the German-Fascist invader and a boundless love towards their mighty motherland, the Soviet Union . . .".

It caused surprise, therefore, when *Izvestiya* on June 26, 1946, published "The Law concerning the Abolition of the Chechen-Ingush Autonomous Soviet Socialist Republic and the Changing of the Crimean Autonomous Soviet Socialist Republic into the Crimean Province", which announced the deportation en masse of the peoples concerned because:

"During the Great Patriotic War, when the people of the USSR were heroically defending the honour and independence of the Fatherland in the struggle against the German-Fascist invaders, many Chechens and Crimean Tatars, at the instigation of German agents, joined volunteer units organized by the Germans and, together with German troops, engaged in armed struggle against units of the Red Army; also at the bidding of the Germans, they formed diversionary bands for the struggle against Soviet authority in the rear; meanwhile, the main mass of the population of the Chechen-Ingush and Crimean ASSRs took no counter-action against these betrayers of the Fatherland."

If this description of the Chechens' actions during the war is even partially accurate it amounts to saying that after twenty years of total isolation from all other influences in their mountain valleys, under what purported to be the most fruitful and satisfying forms of national autonomy, they were ready to take up arms against the régime and to welcome invaders of whom they could have known nothing but the extremely hostile accounts given in the Soviet Press.

Nor was this an isolated case. Of the six autonomous republics of the RSFSR, catering for eight nations, which the Germans reached or (as in the case of the Chechens) merely approached, four were abolished and one cut in half, with the deportation of six of the nations concerned. The Crimean ASSR, the Kalmyk ASSR, the Chechen-Ingush ASSR and the Volga-German ASSR were abolished and their peoples deported, while the Kabardino-Balkar ASSR lost its Balkars. In addition the Karachai Autonomous Province was suppressed and the Karachai were deported. The public announcement of the deportations made in the case of the Checheno-Ingushi and the Crimean Tatars was exceptional. Apart from it there was only a decree of the Supreme Soviet, published in the *Bulletin of the Supreme Soviet of the USSR* of September 2, 1941, announcing the deportation of the Volga-Germans for failing to report the presence of "thousands and tens of thousands of 'diversionists' and spies", so that "the German population of the Volga area conceals enemies of the Soviet people and of Soviet authority in its midst".

The surprising thing is that Moscow should have published even the Chechen decree; a natural conclusion seems to be that encouraging—in Voltaire's sense—the other nations of the Soviet Union appeared more important to the Kremlin than the foreign propaganda aspects of the matter. For nine years under Stalin and three years under his successors no official statement about the majority of these people was ever made.

Apart from the decrees, it is astonishing how far the Soviet Government managed to keep the facts from the world. Even the Chechen and Crimean decree itself was only published retrospectively to cover events which had taken place two years before. In all, populations of at least one million three hundred thousand (on the basis of the population figures for the native inhabitants of these republics given in the *Large Soviet Encyclopedia*) were deported without more than a few hints leaking to the West. Official documents simply ceased to report them, as with the *Soviet Encyclopedia*. Official Soviet maps no longer showed the republics.

Their past was forgotten. There were even direct forgeries: it was stated in the *Encyclopedia* that a "Kabardine Autonomous Soviet Socialist Republic was set up in 1936"—an untruth, since the republic's name then was Kabardino-Balkar. The Soviet *Atlas* for secondary schools contained a map showing the autonomous regions and republics of the Soviet Union in 1922, when several of these areas already had autonomous status. They were shown simply as parts of Russia.

As Mr. Walter Kolarz says, in his *Russia and Her Colonies*, there is no reason why these republics could not have emerged in other areas, if it were simply a question of population transfer. They did not do so. Moreover a list of delegates to the Soviet of Nationalities of the Supreme Soviet of the USSR in 1937 shows that of the 574 delegates there were 10 Volga-Germans, 9 Kalmyks, 5 Chechens, 4 Balkars, 3 Karachai and one Ingush. The list of nationalities represented after the 1950 elections, published in *Izvestiya* on June 15, 1950, showed no representative of any of these nations.

When Khrushchev made his Secret Speech he officially

revealed for the first time the fact of the deportation of most of these people, and he blamed it on Stalin—alleging that the old dictator had wished to deport the Ukrainians as well but found them too large a population to handle in this way. Khrushchev named the Chechens, Ingushi, Balkars, Karachai and Kalmyks. He thus omitted both the Volga-Germans and the Crimean Tatars. Khrushchev stated that the deportations were contrary to communist nationality policy and had had no military justification. He admitted that members of the deported nations had committed "hostile acts" against the Soviet régime, but stated that this was no reason for deporting entire populations. No other communist had previously allowed that even the deportations covered by official decree were more than fairly benevolent transfers to other suitable territories, but Khrushchev now spoke of the "misery and suffering" which had occurred. The five nations mentioned were restored to their rights and their territory by a decree of February, 1957. They are again being criticized for nationalist moods.

Curiously enough, it was claimed by Khrushchev in his speech, and repeated in later Party pronouncements, that the essence of the Soviet Union's nationality policy had been unaffected by Stalin's rule. For example the Central Committee's statement published in *Pravda* on July 2, 1956, says: "no cult of personality could change the nature of the socialist state, which is based on the public ownership of the means of production, the alliance of the working class and the peasantry and the *friendship of the peoples*" (my italics).

The case of the deported nations illustrates most of the contrasts between Soviet paper and Soviet fact. For example, the validity of Soviet elections can be deduced from the fact that in 1938 99·8 per cent of the population of the Volga-German Republic voted and of these 99·7 per cent voted for the government. Three years later they were accused *en masse* of harbouring and failing to report "tens of thousands" of Nazi agents.

Similarly, we are often told that the smaller nations of Russia have enshrined Lenin and Stalin in new folk-lore, expressing the popular feelings. The Kalymk epic, "Yorel", praises Stalin as the creator of a "land of eternal youth, land of eternal abundance" (*Poetry of Kalmykia*, Moscow, 1940). The Chechen "Song of Stalin" exalts him for giving the Chechens happiness and opening for them "the gates to future joy", and goes on to promise that—

> "If the foe shall whet his blade
> Once more, know that we guard our Union;
> Stalin, when you speak the word,
> We shall rend them all like tigers."
> (*Checheno-Ingushi Folk-lore*, Moscow, 1940).

Soviet propaganda had described all these peoples in terms of the ill-treatment they had received at the hands of the Tsars and the wonderful life they enjoyed under the Stalin Constitution. Measures of deportation ordered by the Tsarist Government in 1854 against the Crimean Tatars are denounced in the earlier edition of the *Soviet Encyclopedia*, which also describes a plan to deport the Volga-Germans in 1915 as a "barbarous measure" finally annulled by the October Revolution. The same edition speaks of the Volga-Germans' "limitless devotion" to the cause of Communism and their "rapid progress towards a better, still more joyous, life". It describes a decree of July, 1919, which "underlines the inviolability of Kalmyk territory" and says that the 10th Congress of the Kalmyk Soviets announced in 1931 that "stone by stone the indestructible foundation of the Kalmyk Socialist edifice is being laid". And so on and so forth.

It is clear from these Soviet documents that actions have taken place against the subject races which would have attracted horrified attention on all sides if they had happened anywhere else in the world. The Chechen deportations were carried out by a large MVD task force including the notorious Special Tasks Divisions—DON, headed by Serov (until recently head of Khrushchev's Security Police). It entered Chechnia early in 1944. The entire Chechen-Ingush population, including local Communists, was arrested on the February 22, 1944, at public meetings which had been called ostensibly for the purpose of celebrating Soviet military successes. During the next few weeks scattered resistance was crushed by armed force with thousands of shootings, and the survivors were sent in the customary cattle trucks to various parts of Siberia. Up to 50 per cent are believed to have died of typhus, starvation, and exposure during the long winter journey. They were "resettled" in scattered groups, mixed with other deportees, mainly in labour camps. Immediately after this operation Serov was awarded the Order of Suvorov, usually given to army commanders for victories at the front.

The rounding up of the Karachai, the Kalmyks and the Crimean Tatars, in October, 1943, December, 1943, and June, 1944, respectively, was carried out by the same force, and in similar conditions. The Germans, deported in 1941, seem to have received slightly better treatment. Among other groups suffering deportation, leaving aside the million odd deportees from the Baltic States whose case has been studied in great detail elsewhere, were the Turkish and Greek minorities of the Black Sea littoral.

These were particularly bad cases. In them the nationality policy of which Stalin had even before the revolution been the leading theorist, was tested to destruction. Khrushchev has condemned the particular action, and has restored five out of the seven nations to their earlier rights. The improvement is great. Every credit must be given to the present régime for their return to reasonable normality. If informed Asian opinion has had some effect in producing the result in question, this is also of good augury.

Nevertheless the present system of autonomy is precisely that which produced the tensions which led Stalin to his major crime. The crime itself has been repudiated. But the system is unchanged. And there is no reason to believe that the tensions are very much less. The position now is roughly what it was in the early 'thirties. The significance of the deportations is not so much that it was thought fit to carry them out, as that they constituted absolute proof of the fact that the minority nations were not reconciled to the system which prevailed then and prevails now.

The mutual hostility of these nations and the Soviet régime is not an isolated phenomenon. They incurred their fate merely because they had some opportunity of expressing it. But there is no reason to doubt that the same feelings are nourished by the other subject peoples and in particular the nations of Central Asia, like the Kazakhs, whose numbers dropped by 869,000 between 1926 and 1939, though taking into account the average increase in population in the Soviet Union as a whole there ought to have been an increase of 631,000—that is to say a population deficit over a period of thirteen years of over one and a half million on a total population of three million. It is plain that such peoples suffered considerably more even than the Chechens. Recently Soviet experts have revealed that certain of the small nations of Central Asia, such as the Khakass are in the process of being completely swamped by Russian immigration.

The conflict has been reflected even in the Communist Party itself: a whole series of local Party leaders in all the republics have gone to the firing squad for "bourgeois nationalism" since the late 1920s. Among the few who had a public trial was Faisulla Khodzhayev, Prime Minister of the Uzbek Republic, who confessed to planning "to develop agriculture in Uzbekistan so as to extend grain farming . . . in order to be independent of Russian grain", and other offences of a similar nature. As recently as December, 1958, the Party leader in Turkmenistan, Babaev, has been purged for nationalist excesses.

What, apart from old-fashioned Russian centralism, is the basis for the Soviet leaders' attitude to the minority peoples? Communist theory requires the harnessing of minority nationalist sentiments, first of all against a central authority the Communists wish to destroy, and, secondly, in assisting the Communists in strengthening their own régime. For this purpose the Communists have shown themselves prepared to grant all the *forms* of autonomy and national development that minorities might wish. The cases we have gone into prove that in practice very narrow limitations exist as to what is actually conceded.

The limitation is expressed by Stalin in his report to the 12th Congress of the Communist Party:

"It should be borne in mind that as well as the right of nations to self-determination, there is also the right of the working class to consolidate its power, and to this latter right the right of self-determination is subordinate. There are occasions when the right of self-determination conflicts with the higher right, the right of a working class which has assumed power to consolidate that power. In such cases—this must be said bluntly—the right of self-determination cannot and must not serve as an obstacle to the exercise by the working class of its right to dictatorship."

Stalin's early works, and in particular his writings in the national question, remain official doctrine in spite of the recent attacks on his later behaviour. Nor did this attitude to nationality change with Stalin's death. An article in the authoritative *Kommunist* of October, 1953, on the whole national question in the USSR, is written to the theme "... the national question is subordinate to the more general and fundamental question of the socialist revolution and dictatorship of the proletariat". In other words, national feeling exists to be encouraged or suppressed as the Soviet leaders require.

Nor have attacks on "bourgeois nationalism" ceased even in the most relaxed periods. A new campaign was launched in the first months of 1958, when the Communist Parties of the non-Russian republics of the USSR held their biennial Congresses. All the Party Secretaries appealed for vigilance against ideologies smuggled in by "the enemy". Much of the attack was directed against nationalism. Mustafaev, the First Secretary in Azerbaidzhan, said:

"It is no secret that propaganda hostile to us often tries to play on the national feelings of certain people. We must, therefore, be exceptionally vigilant. Every attempt of hostile elements to undermine the friendship of Soviet peoples, to sow in our midst the poisonous seed of nationalism and chauvinism must be cut short in a most merciless manner."

In all the peripheral republics particular attention was paid to "unhealthy moods" among intellectuals. In Tadzhikistan Uldzhabaev and other Party speakers went to the length of attacking the spreaders of "hostile rumours" and even the circulation of "slanderous and anonymous documents". The campaign was renewed in 1959, when a number of local officials were purged and nationalism was repeatedly denounced.

Khrushchev's closest associate, Aleksander Kirichenko, had earlier delivered a strong attack against "the Ukrainian bourgeois nationalists", whom he denounced as the "henchmen of world reaction". He asserted that the Ukrainian nationalists had been "thoroughly routed". Soviet leaders are usually too realistic to revive ghosts of the past. If they talk, time and again, of the enemy, even of the beaten enemy, they do so in fear of the hidden and surviving moods hostile to the actual centralism of Party rule.

None of the above, it must be repeated, is to beg the question as to whether nationalism (to put it in the simplest and crudest way) is a "progressive" or "reactionary" force. Still less is it to suggest that all non-Communist régimes have been conspicuously successful in solving their nationality problems—the recent history of North Africa stares us in the face. All that we have shown is that, in this particular respect, the Soviet Union has undeniably failed.

CHAPTER X

UNOFFICIAL LIVING

IN A BOOK ABOUT Russia far more must be said about
the State, and about its effects on the ordinary people, than
would be necessary in a book about most other countries.
The State and its multifarious agencies are the context, to an
extent undreamed of here, in which the ordinary man's life
is led. As to the part of life in Russia which does not come
before us in this way, we may say in general that it largely
resembles the ordinary life of ordinary people everywhere.
There is a particular Russian flavour, yet love, family
affection, pleasure, ambition, hatred and suffering work
themselves out in a manner not difficult for us to imagine.
The loving couple or the football crowd in Russia is very like
its equivalent elsewhere.

Beneath the neat conceptions of the Party about the Soviet
Union with its workers, collective farmers and intelligentsia
"building Communism", and practising the Socialist virtues,
lies the vast, untidy unofficial life of the peoples. In the
Soviet press some aspects of it show themselves. These are
naturally enough cases in which the behaviour of the population deviates particularly from the pattern, to the extent that
it is thought necessary to attack it publicly. Those sides of
unofficial life that we are able to describe from Soviet
sources are bound to be largely ones regarded as anti-social.
Some of them *are* anti-social: others, such as addiction to
jazz or religion, would not be thought of as vicious in the
West.

The main difficulty in giving a reasonable picture of the

"anti-social" side is to try to be sure that one is not picking on events which are so rare as to be thoroughly untypical. I have been especially careful, in the following pages, to quote only instances of a type which are reported widely and regularly throughout the Soviet Union. It is true that articles complaining of them often ascribe them to "survivals of capitalism". But this is a form of words used even in cases to which it is hardly applicable—such as that of a seven-year-old alcoholic who stabbed his schoolmaster in Siberia in 1954. Another familiar form of words anyhow often corrects the balance: "Unfortunately this is not an isolated case."

"In the village shop of the Stalin kolkhoz, Lukhovitsi Raion, not long ago there was an interruption in the delivery of sugar and sunflower oil. Instead of waiting for a few days or buying them in Lukhovitsi, where they were available, the kolkhozniks Efimova and Korshunova accepted the offer of the speculator Zolkin to provide them, naturally at a considerable profit" (*Agitator's Notebook*, March, 1957).

This is an absolutely typical complaint. Here we see the cracks in the planned economy being filled spontaneously. Day in and day out the "speculator" is condemned. But he survives ineradicably, and on no small scale. For instance, in November, 1957, there was a long article in the Georgian *Zarya Vostoka* which shows how widespread "speculation" is. It described various arrests and said: "But the catching of one swindler has had no effect whatever on the black market." The Militia (Police) had claimed that there were too many speculators to deal with: "Reference of militia employees to the fact that, they say, there are many speculators and few militiamen, that in this matter the help of all the general public is necessary, cannot be considered unfounded." Not only was the public blamed for its apathy, but even the managers of State shops had not reported speculators who operated openly inside their premises. Some of this trade was of pathetically minor character—the selling of a few eggs, or a few pairs of socks. But there was a great deal of it.

It is also plain that the regular officials who have to administer rulings in practice, and suppress untidy habits of which the Party disapproves, soon begin to show little enthusiasm for the job. This is not a purely Soviet phenomenon. In all Western countries it is notorious that the police are, to put it mildly, extremely lax and inefficient about enforcing laws against prostitution. They have so much else to do, and attempts to enforce the spirit of the law are anyway so lacking in result, that they are inclined to let it go as far as possible unless subjected to heavy pressure from the political authorities. In the Soviet Union such police tasks are on a much wider scale, as there are so many things the Party does not approve of. And although the police is much larger it has so many jobs to cope with, such as internal passport-checking, that it is disinclined to the routine effort of suppressing such things as home brewing and small-scale "speculation". It may look easy to the Party enthusiast, but the policeman knows that large sections of the population are unsympathetic to and unco-operative with the law on the matter.

The way in which the shortages arise are clear enough: "A dispute has been going on for a long time between the factory and the trading organizations about who should supply yeast and where. In particular, the provincial administration of trade considers that the factory is obliged to deliver its products to the towns and districts of the province, and even to deliver it to the shops in the town of Saratov. The director of the factory is absolutely opposed to this. He claims that the factory is obliged to supply its products only to the provincial and Saratov town depots. They are squabbling and the customer suffers. But the speculator makes money. Cannot the Provincial Executive Committee put a stop to this yeast squabble. Of course it can, and the quicker the better.

"It is not only yeast that is subject to speculation. Usually it is simply impossible to buy cotton jeans, children's coats, garden forks, axes and many children's toys. This is a gift to the speculators.

"What was in the mind of the Saratov Council of National Economy when it stopped the production this year of folding beds, tables, chairs, teaspoons and tablespoons, mincing machines and many other household goods?

"Local industries do not always comply with the demands of the trading organizations. For instance, the Glavtorgodezhdi tried for a long time to get the local light industry factories to accept an order for 200,000 pairs of cotton jeans for 1958. There is a big demand for them. But the order was accepted for only 86,000. The surprising thing is that the directors of the Executive Committee agreed. Why? Solely because making the jeans from ordinary cloth is unprofitable.

"It must be admitted that the assortment of goods produced by local and co-operative industry, which was extremely poor anyway, has recently been reduced for some reason. In particular they have stopped making wicker baskets, shopping bags, washing blue and bootlaces.

"It is characteristic that of 237 types of consumer goods dealt with by the trading network. Saratov produces only 52. The others are imported from other parts of the country. It is comic but it is a fact that garden rakes are imported into our Saratov Province from the Baltic Republics, stove dampers from Rostov-on-Don and clothes-pegs from Novosibirsk. Surely all these could be made here!" (*Soviets of Workers Deputies*, No 8, August, 1958).

The extent of illegal trade is sometimes strikingly demonstrated. The Latvian Press in 1957 reported several cases of people arrested for travelling long distances to Riga simply to buy women's woollen scarves. Two men had come from Moscow, and in another case two wholesale *directors* from Kirghizia in Central Asia had been arrested while buying a few scarves in a Riga street when they were supposed to be on a visit to Moscow (*Soviet Latvia*, March 5, 1957).

On September 30, 1956, special decrees were announced against the "unorganized" sale of Georgian foodstuffs outside Georgia. As a result of the new measures, railway trains and cars were searched on the Russian-Georgian frontiers against Georgian contraband. A strict control was also carried out on all planes leaving Georgian airports for Russia proper. It is difficult to realize that the USSR as a whole is working to a unified economic plan.

According to one view, illegal trading is not simply a sign of inefficiency in planning, but a lubrication which makes it possible for the elaborate planned economy to work at all. (The same is said about illegitimate "expense account" items in our present-day highly taxed England.) To plan ordinarily implies to lay down what will actually be done. But in the Soviet Union all enterprises are praised when they "over-fulfil" their plan, while it is common for certain industries to fall short. It is difficult to see how co-ordination can be established. It is as if an engineer who had planned a bridge thought it was all right if some of the piers were higher than the others. At any rate considerable competition for certain materials must occur and shortages must be prevalent as far as official channels are concerned. The director of a factory is thus compelled to seek his materials where he can, unless his whole factory is to grind to a halt, with bad results for the workers and worse for him. It is not to be wondered at that he is inclined to find them where he can, and to bribe and intrigue on the one hand and to purchase on the illegal market on the other.

Bribery is denounced regularly. It often attains huge proportions. The following is a reasonable sample:

"The Prokuratura of the USSR carried out an investigation into systematic bribery and large scale embezzlements in the light industry network in the Estonian and Latvian SSR and also the co-operatives in Leningrad and the Leningrad Province, by means of bribing officials in the supply organizations and industrial undertakings, had received in the course of the last few years more than 170 tons of artificial silk and cloth which were intended to go to textile factories in Estonia and Latvia under the state plan. The artel 'Promvtorsyria' illegally received from the industrial organizations of Tallinn and Riga 33 tons of artificial silk which was under strict rationing. Securing ten times more raw material than it was entitled to under the plan, the artel, by pre-arranged conspiracy with the thieves, passed on a part of the surplus to other artels. Communal property was stolen by various means. In the weaving shop of the artel big surpluses of woven cloth were created by the making out of inflated cutting-out documents. There was no checking system on goods sent out. Bogus invoices were made out and the silk and woollen goods which had not been entered in the records were disposed of through confederates in the trading network. For big bribes officials illegally provided the artels with rationed raw materials. More than two million roubles were paid to 22 officials of the distributing organizations and industrial organizations of Tallinn and Riga for the illegal supply of 172 tons of textile raw materials.

"Instances of bribery, embezzlement and theft which have recently come to light in Kiev, Kharkov and Odessa prove that various co-operative trading associations, when they send the plans for the production of consumer goods to their subordinate artels, societies and minor units, do not interest themselves in how they are stocked with raw materials or the sources from which they obtained them. They themselves often press for illegal issues of raw materials out of the rations of the State industrial undertakings.

"In practice there are frequent cases of bribery where an official has been bribed with embezzled state or communal property, and a crime of this kind cannot be regarded merely as a case of bribery" (*Socialist Legality*, No. 12, December, 1958).

That was a major operation. The ordinary individual bribe is often heard of too, as when "Zaturenski, Chief Mechanic of the 'Elektromontazh' Trust (Minsk), in order to secure housing accommodation more quickly, came into the office of the manager of the Trust and handed him an envelope containing 1,000 roubles." The Prokuror of the October Raion of the town of Minsk refused to start a prosecution on the grounds that 'Zaturenski offered a bribe because he was illiterate and backward, as a result of a survival of the past'. "It is difficult to understand why the Raion Prokuror should decide that the Chief Mechanic of a Trust, who had received a secondary education, was illiterate, or why any survivals of the past in his mind should free him from prosecution." This case also shows the reluctance of officialdom to proceed too, except when prodded by the party enthusiast.

Another major problem is the faking of plan fulfilment returns, as in a recent complaint in a high Party organ: "The same thing happens with poultry. In our kolkhoz we have 400 laying hens. In February or March last year we took 1,000 chicks from the incubator station. In August-September the young hens began to lay, but their eggs were included as being the output of the 400 old hens. That is how a 'high' egg yield is obtained. . . . It is a great pity that the party organization of the district does not wage a war against eyewash. I work as manager of the poultry farm of the kolkhoz. I find myself in a dilemma. If I record the egg yield properly, I shall appear as lagging behind the other poultry farms. If I follow the example of other people, I shall appear dishonestly as one of the best" (*Party Life*, August, 1958).

Khrushchev has spoken strongly on alcoholism, but there is little to show whether there is more of it or less than in Tsarist times, or in present-day Russia than elsewhere. It is now attacked more frequently than any other "social" vice. Drinking as a major entertainment has often gone with a shortage of other ways, or other tolerable ways, of passing the time. The rise of alcoholism to be a major evil in Poland after the war is now admitted to have been due very largely to this: the Polish poet Wazyk speaks of the inhabitants of the new workers' settlements as "bestial with vodka" because "howling with boredom". Russian drinking habits have always been described as rather different from those of the Western-type alocholic, and are apparently much less unhealthy. Rather than semi-permanent addiction, they go in for one colossal blind every month or so.

The Russian attitude to drink is not an easy one for the State to change. At the height of Khrushchev's campaign a waiter in a Moscow restaurant was refusing to accept the answer, "No, nothing thank you," when he had asked, "What you want to drink?" In a very amusingly written feuilleton in *Komsomolskaya Pravada* of January 14, 1958—not on alcohol at all, but on the complete prevalence everywhere of the supposedly abolished habit of demanding tips—the waiter retorts, "This is a restaurant not a canteen, you know! *So what will you drink?*" ("The waiter pronounces this in a

loud voice deliberately so that everyone around will hear.")
In an earlier campaign one of the customs denounced was
that anybody in a grocer's shop wanting vodka automatically
goes to the head of the queue.

The State makes a very large profit on alcohol. A litre
bottle of vodka costs 86 kopeks to produce and sells at 60
roubles, a profit of about 7,000 per cent. During one of the
campaigns against alcoholism a few years ago, various
opinions appeared in the Press which gave the impression
that the habit of drinking oneself silly was not only widespread, but also widely respected. The youth papers complained in various connections about almost every main
trade that young workers entering it were told: "You
cannot be a real miner (or foundry worker, or forester, or
whatever it happened to be) unless you can drink." Illegal
distilling was reported from scores and scores of presumably representative villages—though cases were sometimes
selected for their extreme shamelessness, as in one where the
main illicit still was specially distinguished by being clearly
visible not only from the office of the local Soviet, but from
those of the Party and the Police as well!

An account of the situation in Rostov-on-Don showed the
disadvantages of the youth organizations in their campaign,
which was contested at every step by the organs of the
Ministry of Internal Trade. At one Rostov factory, while
there was not a bookshop for several miles, dozens of vodka-
selling establishments lay within that radius. Many of these
were supposed to sell ice-cream, eggs and various other
consumer goods, but at all of them it was extremely difficult
to get anything but drink. Their employees explained that it
was far easier to meet their plan and get a high turnover by
selling vodka, which required no nonsense like cooking. The
Young Communist League finally managed to stop the
works' canteen selling vodka to young workers inside the

factory, but the canteen management riposted by selling it to them through a window on to the street, claiming that this was outside the factory's jurisdiction. Finally, the Rostov youth officials were horrified, on turning up at their offices one day, to find that the ground floor had opened up as a dram shop.

If combatting the legal trade is difficult, it is at least attempted by young enthusiasts. The campaign against illegal distilling has to be conducted by the regular police, who do not greatly care about it. The authorities in 1958 complained that the police "often displayed very little keenness and sometimes remained completely inactive". Some of them had even worked out a series of quibbles proving that it was not illegal and in certain regions not a single prosecution had been brought for a year, in spite of numbers of cases being known. As an authoritative voice points out, the lower courts even retain the Russian's soft spot for a drunkard in cases like the following:

"Loginov, working as manager of a shop in the village of Nalinsk, systematically appropriated co-operative funds and drank, in this way embezzling more than 7,000 roubles. The People's Court, in the judgement, gave as its reason for applying to Loginov a sentence lighter than the one indicated by law the fact that 'Loginov had spent the money in drinking and had not pursued the objectives of gain'. Clearly, such an approach to the case does not contribute in any degree to the proper organization of the struggle with pilfering in selling organizations" (*Sovietskaya Yustitsiya*, July, 1958).

The ingenuity shown in illegal operations like home distilling is well illustrated by a story that appeared in *Evening Moscow* in February, 1959. A woman who worked in the Moscow Zoo was found to have misappropriated the food of elephants and monkeys, as material for an illegal distillery.

When her flat was searched several hundredweight of grain and sugar was found, together with over 100 bottles of 90% proof spirit.

Various types of problem youth, many of them of the teddy-boy type, are regularly denounced in the Soviet Press. Some seem to be untypical eccentrics, like the young man in Orel who removed his shirt in a tram to reveal an obscene tattooing. But certain complaints are general. A new one has developed in the last few years, against the *Nibonicho*. *Nibonicho* is an abbreviation of the Russian words: *ni boga ni chorta* (neither god nor devil):

"Where do they spring from, these haughty parasites and sceptics with a contemptuously protruding lip, who by their entire behaviour and appearance stress that there is nothing sacred for them in life? Who are these characters who either put on serious airs when everyone around them is having fun, or insolently mock at everything when people around them are stirred. They do not necessarily wear super-long jackets or ultra-short trousers. They are dressed modestly and do not sport any extravagant haircuts. In a word, their appearance encourages confidence. More than that, they themselves usually despise teddy-boys and crack a joke at their expense. They try not to attract attention, preferring, so to say, to merge with the mass and to stir up trouble on the quiet.

"A debate, let us say, is arranged in a school where Komsomol members want to talk about happiness. The floor is taken by youths and girls; they are excited, speak in the best way they can, enter into arguments. From a distant, dimly-lit corner of the hall, once in a while, in response to the excited and sincere words of the speaker, there comes a remark:

" 'Hear that? . . . Pa-tri-ot-ism!'

"Immediately someone else, hiding behind the backs of others, will utter in the same tone:

" 'Stormy ovation! All rise!'

"This is the local *nibonicho* crowd at work.

"This outward bravado can deceive only youngsters to whom such coxcombs may appear as 'independent-thinking personalities'. But, coming constantly in contact with young people, I gladly see how both in schools and colleges the foul essence of such pseudo-daredevils is being gradually exposed" (*Literary Gazette*, May 25, 1957).

The rich *stilyag*—spoiled, stylishly dressed, living a life of idle dissipation—has long been a common target for the caricaturist, though it seems that it has been impossible to drive the type out of existence by shame, or by any other method. An example of the way in which they feel themselves exempt from duties was given when some children of medium-rank officials were arrested for robbery: "It never occurred to any of them that they would have to work in a factory or on a construction site. They were confident that they were created for a different sort of life. The parents themselves instilled this idea in their children. Alla [one of the miscreants] confessed that her stepfather, Lt-Col. Kolesov, once said:

" 'If you behave badly, I shall go to the militia and ask them to send you to the virgin lands.'

"What a sacrilegious ring these words have!" (*Komsomolskaya Pravda*, August 15, 1958).

The magazine *Sovetskaya Kultura* said on January 18, 1955: "Girl *stilyagi* wear dresses stretched tightly over their figures to the point of indecency. The skirts are slit and their lips are highly painted. In the summer they wear 'Roman' sandals, their hair being done in the style of fashionable foreign actresses. These so-called 'dynamic play-girls' amuse themselves by going with chance acquaintances to restaurants and being treated to meals, which they repay with promising glances."

Under the title "Butterflies", *Trud* of April 24, 1954, has described at some length the life of Moscow women who "willingly devoted their evenings to an easy restaurant life . . . hoping to pick up some prosperous old man with a beaver collar who did not grudge 'money for entertainment' ". There are occasionally other more open references to prostitution—but this is a subject about which a citizen of London may be excused from expatiating.

The passion of these, but also of admittedly respectable young people as well, is for jazz. In August, 1958, *Pravda*, in an article, "Eradicate Vulgarity in Music", attacked variety orchestras which resort to a cunning device of occasionally performing "in the guise of parodies of rock and roll . . . ugly examples of that very kind of unbridled music" which they are ostensibly guying. *Izvestiya* on September 28, 1958, complained: "jazzomania is assuming the character of a chronic illness, and it must be cured by serious public intervention. . . . There are theoreticians among us who see in jazzomania the spirit of the times and who completely fail to take into consideration the harmfulness of the influence of the formalistic, bourgeois art form. . . ."

An article in *Sovietskaya Yustitsiya* (September, 1958) during the music-purification drive revealed that it is already a punishable offence to "produce home-made records of a criminally-hooligan trend". The article recounts how a young man resorted to participation in a murder so as to buy records made illegally on X-ray plates. The corrupting records were of the "latest rock-and-roll, gypsy songs, scurrilous ditties from the criminal world, and drum solos by American jazz kings". This trade in illicit records is also described in a long letter in *Komsomolskaya Pravda* (October

15, 1958) headed "Melodies in Short Supply", which described how X-ray plate records are peddled for exorbitant sums in Kuibyshev market.

The Party find vulgarity on the variety stage also. The purification offensive began in the *Pravda* article, "Disseminators of Vulgarity", already referred to. An example of "vulgarity" considered particularly obnoxious is given of a writer, not untalented, who after "singing the praises of the stars and the Soviet sputniks" in his script, "descended into the quagmire of vulgarity" by making a joke asserting that "each one of us who is married . . . first of all found out whether the girl had a room and whether she earned good money". This joke, says the article, is a slander on all Soviet married men, inasmuch as it attributes to them "petty bourgeois" and "predatory" motives.

Gamblers are attacked from time to time, as with the gang that insolently played right under the shadow of the Bolshoi Theatre in mid-Moscow. But articles on them are rare. On the other hand, beggars are regularly censured. The following is a typical account:

> "From the old days we have inherited such shameful features as tramps and beggars. How often does each one of us see scenes like this: Beggars in groups or singly slink from carriage to carriage of a suburban train, and you hear a voice, hoarse from over-indulgence in drink, whining 'Spare something for a man who suffered for you in the war.' The Soviet man is responsive and sensitive and money pours generously into the cap of the 'disabled soldier'. In the course of a day such a 'sufferer' collects 200 roubles or more.

> "Vladislav Troinikovski has been in the Perov collection point No. 1 on many occasions after a bout of drunkenness and disorder. He is a young fellow, born in 1931, but

has already been in prison for robbery. In a drunken brawl his hand was shattered and had to be amputated. But Troinikovski was not dismayed. He immediately got hold of a uniform and struck on a row of medal ribbons bought in a shop. The fact that one of them was the medal for 'Mother heroines' did not bother him. The public would not look too closely. So now at the railway stations and in trains you can hear: 'Spare something for one who suffered for you in the war.'

"M. L. Movikov, born in 1877, lives on the Stromynka and receives a pension as a retired worker. Two sons and two daughters pay him 800 roubles a month. You would imagine it ought to be enough for the old man. But you can often see him about the streets begging for alms. Probably many of the passers-by think, 'Poor old man, one must do something to help him.' And this 'unfortunate' has more than 30,000 roubles in his savings book.

"F. Erokhina travels regularly to Moscow from the Kaluga Province 'to work'. In the country she has her own brick house and a nice plot of land, a cow, a pig, several dozen geese, etc. But having dressed herself in rags, she stands at the station approach and whines, 'Spare something for a fire victim.'

"Don't give it! Such gifts only breed idlers." (*Agitators' Notebook*, October, 1957.)

A final disreputable practice, from the Soviet point of view, is religion. On the basis of sales of candles, it is reckoned that there are between twenty and thirty million practising members of the Orthodox Church. The Lutheran Church of Estonia claims 700,000 active members, that of Latvia 600,000, and the Baptist congregations all over Russia have at least 550,000 baptized members and, according to their own estimates, about 3,000,000 sympathizers.

The Party members themselves are blamed for the state of affairs. For example:

"Some village communists have not yet become militant, active fighters against religious prejudices. They agree that such prejudices are harmful for the cultural development of the people and for the economy, but they do not go beyond that. There are even some who have no objection to having a drink 'in honour of the Holy Ghost'. In the Pobeda kolkhoz the Communist Alexandrov even tried to give this a legal sanction. 'The Soviet Constitution gives freedom of conscience to everybody, so I am going to celebrate,' he announced to the Secretary of the Party organization" (*Party Life*, January, 1959).

Boredom is also alleged to drive people into Churches, though when on February 19, 1957, "*Komsomolskaya Pravda*" printed a complaint from Stalino, that some young workers of the Stalin Metallurgical Factory often went to morning service after night-shift, this reason would scarcely apply.

Even children are affected. K. D. Radina, in a pamphlet, *Atheist Education of Children in the Family* (Leningrad, 1955), stated that in some cases "children live a double life, adjust themselves and manœuvre between the demands of school and family, conceal their religious views from their teachers and comrades, hide their crucifixes, and grow accustomed to insincerity, deceit and falsehood".

Odd Millenarian sects are also regularly reported as raising their heads in various parts of the Soviet Union. In 1957 a group called Innokentiites were denounced in Moldavia. They had claimed that one of their members was the Grand Duke Alexei, the last Tsar's son. There are also frequent outbreaks of amulet-selling, holy springs and so on.

Dozens and dozens of reports resemble complaints that in the Kuibyshev Province sectarian preachers and all sorts of "holy men" were at work to deceive the people.

In November, 1957, there began a new wave of strong attacks on various sects. Jehovah's Witnesses were accused of making converts and of inculating an anti-Soviet spirit on the basis, "Our State is not from God; therefore it must perish". Adventists were also attacked for "sabotage" in that they banned participation in public life. The Baptists "slander the Soviet way of life, the Communist Party and our policy, but they frequently disguise themselves and pretend to be innocent. Moreover, they have even declared their god Jesus was of proletarian origin and even socialist and communist."

The Jehovah's Witnesses were active in Taishet, and were recruiting a number of young people. Taishet used to be a major labour camp centre during the Stalin period, and the local propagandists of the Witnesses are simply former camp inmates who, having been amnestied, are now propagating their faith among the local population. The same thing is happening in other former labour camp areas, and largely accounts for the astonishing spread of strange sects in the most unexpected parts of the Soviet Union, especially in Kazakhstan. Ex-convicts returning to European Russia spread the infection. A long article printed on May 25, 1958, in the Byelorussian Communist paper, *Sovetskaya Byelorussia*, entitled "Who is Hiding behind Ancient Jehovah?", complains about proselytizing activities of a thirty-four-year-old Byelorussian, who on his return from a prison camp was spreading the Jehovah's Witness creed among his fellow-villagers.

On May 15, 1958, the central organ of the Communist Party of Tadzhikistan printed an article entitled "Carriers of Darkness", denouncing the activities of Baptists and Seventh Day Adventists in Stalinabad, the Tadzhik capital. The paper's main grievance that both sects recruited members from among the Soviet intelligentsia. Of those who had become attracted to the Seventh Day Adventists, the paper listed the technological expert of the Stalinabad furniture factory, a young woman who had graduated from the Mathematics and Physics Faculty of Stalinabad State University, and, finally, three advanced students of the Stalinabad Medical Institute. The paper was particularly incensed about the religious conversion of the medical students.

Sovetskaya Byelorussia of May 30, 1958, gave an interesting example of revival. It mentioned a Byelorussian village church not far from the Soviet-Polish border which, until 1956, seemed to be in a state of total decay. Then a new parish priest arrived, who invited young people in the church and taught them to play musical instruments. After a few months, in the spring of 1957, he had assembled sufficient supporters to be able to collect money for the repair of his church.

Islam and Islamic practices like Ramadan similarly raise their heads obstinately in the Asian republics, and are as regularly attacked.

The number of Russians who practise one or other of these social vices—speculation, bribery, alcoholism, jazz, begging, scepticism and religion—must cover a very large section indeed of the population. In fact, it seems likely that few are exempt from one or other of these sins. This may tend to show that, human nature being what it is, the power of the Party to impose conformity is in practice a highly qualified one. This failure is a radical one, and relevant to both the strength and the permanence of the grip of the régime's ideas upon the population.

CHAPTER XI

WRONG IDEAS: THE WRITERS

IF WE WANT TO see the nature of unofficial thought and feeling in the USSR, our most sensible course is to examine what was said during the brief period when some expression of them was allowed. This was the time between Khrushchev's Secret Speech at the 20th Party Congress in February, 1956, and the gradual suppression of almost all unorthodox manifestations which got into its swing in the autumn and winter of 1956 and was almost complete a year later—though attacks on the peccant views continue unabated.

This was the period when the cellar door was lifted, at least slightly, for the first time for many years. And though it has shut again, there is every reason to believe that the ideas remain the same, even though they can no longer be expressed. What was said in 1956 can reasonably stand for what is thought in 1959 or 1960.

It is not that any large scale license was granted to heretical views even during this period: for instance, *Dr. Zhivago* could not secure publication, even in censored form. Still, it nearly did. And, quite a lot of fairly heterodox material came out. While it would be perfectly reasonable to speculate that there was a good deal more that the Russians would have given tongue about if they could have, we are at least on certain and undeniable ground when we look at what is actually there for all to read. The fact that a lot of work finally condemned as incorrect was published—even though it was publicly criticized at the time—does not appear to mean that the mechanics of control in literature slackened, so much as that certain Party members, even in high places, were willing to allow some true relaxation as part of the repeal of the Stalin line. For instance, Shepilov was afterwards accused of allowing too much latitude to the writers, "with the result that certain demagogic elements among the artistic intelligentsia had the chance of indulging themselves to the limit".

It is certainly true that a ferment of new thought appeared in the lower ranks of the Party as such. These were seldom referred to, but it was said that "Such opinions as those which are objectively directed towards the dethroning of the leadership chosen by the Party masses themselves, and towards the discrediting of Party cadres, have nothing in common with a correct Leninist understanding of the role of leaders. Such opinions have been expressed by individual, insufficiently politically mature Communists in discussing the results of the 20th Congress. . . . In the course of discussion questions were asked: Why did prominent leaders, during the period of the cult of the individual, not come out against it openly? Is not this proof of a lack of personal courage?" (*Kommunist*, July, 1956).

The same paper later referred to a particular case:

"When, at the meeting of the Party organization of a scientific laboratory, a small group of workers, under cover of a discussion about the personality cult, tried to exploit inner-Party democracy for slander against the Party and attacks against its policy, the Central Committee of the CPSU took a stern decision, not only against that group, but also against the Party organization as a whole, which did not repel the slanderers" (*Kommunist*, December, 1957).

In the literary field things showed themselves far more strongly, or at least got more publicity. Literary debate overlapped indeed into politics, as when: "In one of his speeches, the writer Pokrovsky declared that a tribe of bureaucrats had seized power in our country. He was referring to the leading cadres of the party and the State . . ." (Ryurikov, Head of the Culture and Science Department of the Central Committee, quoted in the Report of a Delegation of Italian Communists, Editori Riuniti, Rome, 1958).

The 1956-7 thaw produced a number of writers who had not been heard of before. The debates centred on names like Yashin, Evtushenko, Granya and Dudintsev. Party spokesmen attacked this new writing as having "a special flavour" —the main ingredient of which was said to be "pessimism". But there is little of what we would think of as pessimism in it: what is meant seems to be a refusal to see everything hallowed by the Party as rosy.

The movement occurred both among the young and among the prizewinners of the Stalin generation, like Aliger and Panova. Many of the writers were Party members. They wrote within the Soviet system, demanding only truth and freedom to speak it, implying a Communist régime reformed, but not revolutionized. They assume the possibility of a humanized Soviet state.

They are thus not comparable to Pasternak, for whom the Soviet system, like politics in general, is transitory and episodic. Pasternak is widely recognized in Soviet literary circles for his overshadowing talents, and his return to the deeper sources of human feeling is in accord with the new mood as it is with the old Russian spirit, but he is not typical of the present ferment as far as ideas or struggles are concerned. His case is widely known, and I will not cover it.

In January, 1957, *Literary Gazette* published an article which contained this significant passage:

"We have heard voices which incorrectly interpret the conception of 'freedom of thought', 'freedom of literature', and so on. We are by no means supporters of any kind of freedom . . . which is contrary to the principles of Party allegiance and Communist ideology."

Regular attacks began to appear on the magazine *Novy Mir* and the anthology, *Literary Moscow*. The latter was to prove the chief bone of contention at the plenum of the Moscow branch of the Union of Writers, held in March. One of its editors, Kaverin, counter-attacked. *Literary Gazette* of March 19, 1957, noted that "V. Kaverin showed complete intolerance of criticism, although he himself did not curb his expressions, and even threatened his opponents with legal action".

Dudinstev, too, defended himself with spirit and to good effect. He represented his critics as men striking angrily with a stick. "I think," he said, "we might be allowed, as young swimmers are, to attempt to swim alone. After all, we might not drown! But alas, I constantly feel around me that lead which is at times used for guiding infants. And it hinders me from swimming. . . ."

He also gave some indications of why he had written *Not by Bread Alone*. He reminded his critics that he had fought during the war. "I was lying in a trench," he said, "and an air battle was going on over my head. The Messerschmitts were shooting down our aircraft, which in fact outnumbered them greatly. At that moment a kind of split occurred in me, because until then I had always heard that our aircraft were better and faster than any others."

The implication was clear: he had felt compelled to speak out against the sort of thing that made this possible.

Not by Bread Alone was published in serial form in *Novy Mir* of August, September and October, 1956. The 140,000 copies of *Novy Mir* sold like nylons. The interest in it was so intense that at a discussion held at the Writers' House in Moscow the auditorium was packed to overflowing, and young people climbed stepladders and poked their heads in through the windows. *Literary Gazette* referred to Dudintsev as one of the authors who had "lost their sense of proportion in denouncing vice". *Izvestia* denounced the book as a "failure", and expressed fears about the "unhealthy agitation" which it had aroused. *Kommunist* remarked that Dudintsev had "lost his sense of perspective, got into a panic and exaggerated the danger, presenting bureaucracy in our conditions as an impenetrable brick wall. . . .".

From the point of view of professional novel-writing technique, a number of books of the Stalin era were far better written. But Soviet readers seemed to find that even rather a plain child had more life in it than the most exquisitely constructed puppet.

The errant writers were clearly patriotic. In fact in a sense their truth and their patriotism were one. Kirsanov's allegorical poem, "Seven Days of the Week", was strongly attacked. But its essence is simply a call for a new and nobler heart for Russia. Another poem much censured was the twenty-three-year-old Evtushenko's "Zima Station". He describes squalor as well as happiness in his home village in Siberia, and believes the message to be:

"Truth is good and happiness better,
But without truth there is no happiness,"

Another story in *Literary Moscow*, "The Levers", by Yashin, depicts the brutalization of human beings as soon as they act solely as instruments of the Party. Yet another, "Visit to the Home Town", exposes the faults of the collective farm system. *Literary Gazette* described the whole thing, during the Moscow debate, by the now stereotyped phrase, "unhealthy agitation".

Another Soviet novel of this Thaw, *The Difficult Campaign*, by Lyubov Kabo, shows the children of a Soviet secondary school turning against various things in Soviet life: the way events are reported in the press, which one of the children calls "lies"; the chauvinism which imposes words like "City bread" and "Southern nuts" for the usual "French bread" and "American nuts"; the system of Stalin Prizes, and the generally false picture given in Soviet literature. One child compares the collective farms in Sholokov's *Virgin Soil Upturned* with his own experience at his uncle's kolkhoz, where the peasants still sometimes get no pay for their work days "even now, seven years after the war". This book is different from others in that it has a "real" Communist, a teacher who attracts the children's loyalty by a philosophy of brotherhood unlike that of the Party officials.

That the writers exhibited solidarity, that an intellectual opinion had built up outside the official views was strongly alleged (as it still is from time to time). A leader in *Pravda* of May 19, 1957, referred to "individual writers, who, having forgotten their high civic calling, for demagogic purposes created a clamour around works which were devoid of artistic merit and which gave a false impression of life; writers who engaged in unprincipled agitation in gratification of petty group interests".

At the May, 1957, Conference of the Board of the Writers' Union, the rebels practised silence. Speaker after speaker demanded that they should come forward and address the meeting. Members of the Moscow group who had spoken out two months before were challenged by name. "It is well known," said Sobolev, an official speaker, "that V. Dudintsev's novel has become a kind of banner. And . . . some people intended to make the collection *Literary Moscow* a a similar kind of banner. But a banner has to be defended. It has surprised me that the writers who are making this collection their banner . . . have not come on to the rostrum of the plenum and defended their position. . . . Your silence is dangerous; it misleads the reading public. What does it mean? What does it hide?"

At a meeting of Leningrad writers in June, 1957, two other anthologies were mentioned: *Literary Tribune* and *The Breaking Wave*. *Literary Gazette* said that the former was "unsatisfactory" and "some of its material had to be removed because it was ideologically weak". The report added that "it was only due to the intervention of the Secretariat and the Party bureau" that the situation was "put right". The Editor of *The Breaking Wave*, took the almost unprecedented step, in Soviet conditions, of resigning rather than put up with such interference from the Party. She was the fifty-two-year-old Vera Panova, a three-times Stalin prize-winner and one of the most popular Soviet authors today.

Suppressed tastes began to emerge with the withdrawal of criminal charges against authors long since purged. The Party's literary chief, Surkov, complained in *Literary Gazette* on November 28, 1957:

"If a few years ago there was silence about the experience of, for example, such figures of literature and art as V. Meyerhold, A. Tairov, B. Pilnyak, M. Bulgakov, I. Babel, and others [all shot or died in camps in the 'thirties and 'forties] in recent times some critics and theatre experts have dashed to the other extreme, exaggerating the significance of the creative experience of these theatrical and literary figures, amnestying in a wholesale manner their real mistakes and errors. There were attempts to canonize the creations of B. Pasternak and some other contemporary poets close to him in tendency. M. Tsvetaeva [committed suicide in prison, 1940] was noisily raised almost to the rank of the most outstanding Russian poet of the first half of the twentieth century. The attacks against socialist realism, as can be seen from the above examples, were accompanied by attempts to revive, as something that was positive experience, that which had been judged and condemned already in the creative discussions of the 'twenties and early 'thirties."

A Soviet summary of the events of the abortive movement towards a freer art is clear and full: "However, certain writers . . . have cut themselves off from the life of the people and do not understand their vital interests. . . . By their waverings and their confused rushes in all directions, such ideologically unstable writers and artists only hinder the real struggle for a further development of Soviet culture. They tried to take advantage of the criticism of the personality cult started by the Central Committee of the Communist party in order to undertake a revision of all the basic decisions of the party in the sphere of literature, art and aesthetics, and called for the abandonment of the principles of Party spirit, of the spirit of the people, of the links between art and literature and life, on the grounds that allegedly they were outdated. They opposed the Party direction of art and literature and they opposed Socialist realism as being a method which had allegedly been discredited from above" (*Questions of Philosophy*, No. 6, 1957).

The intervention of the Party was massive and repeated. "A report on these unwholesome tendencies was submitted to the Central Committee, and the Central Committee requested the best elements among the writers themselves to conduct a struggle against such tendencies. Indeed, when Dudintsev made a mistaken intervention in defence of his own book, *Not by Bread Alone*, many well-known writers criticized him. With this aim in view, two meetings were convened by the Central Committee, one in December and the other in May, and Khrushchev, Pospelov and the writers themselves exposed these unwholesome tendencies to sharp criticism" (Report of the Italian Communist Delegation, Rome, 1958).

Suggestions about the right sort of literature continued,

the youth papers being particularly incensed at the treatment of their fledgling politicos, with such comments as:

"The Secretary of the Moscow City Committee, Comrade
Pavlov, expressing the opinion of the activists who were
present, said: 'We are amazed at the tendency of certain
producers, scenario writers and playwrights to draw com-
parisons between Komsomol activists and workers and so-
called ordinary people (as though the former were not
ordinary people). In these films and plays the ordinary lads
and girls at least bear a resemblance to normal people, but
the youth leaders, the Komsomol activists, are invariably
hidebound bureaucrats, formalists and fools. . . . And really,
the figure of the activist migrates from book to book, from
play to play, from film to film, and always wearing the same
silly mask of a bureaucrat, a colourless, stupid person"
(*Molodoi Kommunist*, April, 1958).

At the same time another youth paper, *Komsomolskaya
Pravda*, gave its idea of the right type of hero. It complained
that Soviet authors of adventure stories never give a proper
picture of the secret policemen—the "Chekists"—and their
close ties with the people. As a result, a Soviet boy or girl
or even an adult would be hard put, said *Komsomolskaya
Pravda*, to write an essay on "A Portrait of a Communist-
Chekist".

During the partial "Thaw" of 1953-4 the critic
Pomerantsev was attacked with extreme bitterness in the
Party organs. He had gone to the length of claiming that
"sincerity" was the mark of the true writer, the thing that
distinguishes "the author of a book from the compiler of a
book". Pomerantsev was expressing in simple terms the fact
that a writer who follows orders, or even his own political
convictions, when his imagination is not naturally engaged,
is going to produce worthless hack work. *Literary Gazette*
retorted that "the first test for a Marxist" was not sincerity,

but "evaluation of the ideological-artistic quality of the work". We must conclude that, if this be so, a Marxist cannot be a true writer. But is it so? Marx himself spoke against any attempt to put political pressure on poets. What is at issue here is not the fact that the Party is a Communist Party. The particular organization of society for which it speaks is irrelevant. For the trouble is less in the content of its politics than in their extent.

Though the literary and artistic troubles made the biggest news in the outside world, the Party was at least equally concerned with an outburst of "bourgeois objectivity" among historians. The leading historical magazine *Questions of History* started to fill the vacuum left by Khrushchev's announcement that the current histories were fakes, with spirited attempts to investigate the original facts. The Assistant Editor, Burdzhalov, produced or sponsored much in this line which went against the grain. The main fields in which trouble was caused were the history of the Party in 1917 and the nature of the Tsarist wars of annexation in the Caucasus. On the former the historians began to dig out facts about how individual Bolshevik leaders had actually conducted themselves. On the Caucasus, a number of writers, and speakers at historians' conferences, not only demolished the Stalinist view that the Tsarist conquest of the Caucasus was progressive, but substituted for it the claim that Caucasian resistance had been a normal national-liberation struggle against imperialism. One historian went to the length of saying that history should not be "politics projected into the past". After a long-drawn-out series of arguments, in which the Editorial Board was subjected to pressure by the Agitation and Propaganda Department of the Central Committee, and finally by the Secretariat itself, the deviant lines were suppressed and the Editorial Board was purged. Winding up the debate, *Kommunist* (March, 1957) accused *Questions of History* of "the distortion of questions which were decided long ago and which were not subject to any kind of doubt". *Kommunist* added that "any attempt to hide a disregard for a Party spirit, any spurious regard for 'objectivity' in the analysis of social events, will not stand up to criticism". What is more, the historians, even after their views had been attacked in *Pravda* and *Kommunist*, "did not find the courage to admit errors they had committed"—a curious way of putting it, to say the least.

Burdzhalov was condemned in the *Bulletin of the Academy of Sciences* of May, 1957, in the following terms:

"In the article 'On the tactics of the Bolsheviks in March-April, 1917", published in No. 4 for 1956, and also in speeches at readers' conferences, the deputy editor-in-chief, Candidate of Historical Sciences E. N. Burdzhalov, under the guise of criticism of the personality cult, tried to stress the part played by Zinoviev in 1917, treating questions of the ideological and political struggle of our party in an objectivistic spirit."

The fact that history is not open to debate was further made clear: "Unfortunately, some historians have shown an irresponsible approach to the problems before them and have published in the Press reconsiderations of isolated questions which had already been decided by our Marxist historical scholarship" (*Bulletin of the Moscow University*, No. 2, 1957).

A truly crucial example of the distinction between various ideas about what constitutes legitimate freedom of opinion appeared in the authoritative *Party Life* of January, 1958, in an article by a prominent official of the Central Committee. At Leningrad University two students of the Literary Union of the Philological Faculty "spoke incorrectly" in connection with a poem of a friend. The Director declared that they were "on the other side of the barricade"; they were shouted at, they were threatened. But when the Rector of the

University came and talked with these students simply, "in a comradely manner", they confessed their mistakes. The Director who hectored the students was acting as a Stalinist. The Rector who argued them out of their views in a friendly manner represents the theory, at least, of the Party's present methods. But the story also shows the continuing absence of any notion that a third solution is permissible: that the students might be allowed to keep their opinions, that, in fact, "correctness" may have no meaning, and if it does it cannot be assumed to be the possession of the authorities.

The creative minds of Russia showed, when the brief opportunity arose, that they did not share the official view. They no longer speak out so freely, but attacks on their known opinions still continue to be made. It would appear, then that, after decades of regimentation, there is still a good deal of freedom in writers' minds, if not in their pens: and, in estimating Soviet potentialities, this freedom, however precarious, must be taken into account, as well as the regimentation.

CHAPTER XII

WRONG IDEAS: THE STUDENTS

"THE WESTERLY WIND often blows the putrid miasmas of bourgeois degeneration into our country. Unhardened organisms are most susceptible to their influence. Some youths, who have not yet seen anything of life and can hardly grow a moustache, discuss art or even the imperfections of the era in a tone of a prophet" (*Pravda Ukrainy*, May 16, 1957). Such is a typical comment of the period. In fact, the students had exercised the notorious prerogative of students the world over. They had begun to think.

Komsomolskaya Pravda, the official organ of the Young Communists, spoke of student-speakers "attacking the achievements of our Socialist camp", and of statements "intended to impress the imagination of the audience by their boldness". The students even went to the length of producing illicit periodicials, some of which were named:

The Fig Leaf	an illegal publication by Vilnius University students in Lithuania (*Komsomolskaya Pravda*, December 23, 1955).
The Azure Bud	illegal publication of Leningrad University students (*Komsomolskaya Pravda*, January 4, 1956).
Culture	a wall newspaper published by students in the Leningrad Technological Institute (*Komsomolskaya Pravda*, December 4, 1956).
Fresh Voices	a manuscript magazine published by

	students of the Obrastsov Railway Transport Institute in Leningrad (*Komsomolskaya Pravda*, December 16, 1956).
Heresy	a manuscript journal produced by students of the Krupskaya Bibliotechnical Institute in Leningrad (*Komsomolskaya Pravda*, December 28, 1956).
The Bell	a wall newspaper produced by students of Moscow University (*Moskovskiy Universitet*, December 4, 1956).

The largest of all universities in the USSR is the Lomonosov University in Moscow. Students there appear to have been expelled for producing bulletins of BBC and other foreign news broadcasts during the Hungarian Revolution. The University newspaper published an account at the beginning of December, 1956, of a University Party Organization meeting at which the students were taken to task for "alien views", expressed in the language of fables in wall newspapers like *The Bell*. There were also stormy student meetings inside the University. Those held in private are said to have been the scene of the most forthright "demands". But even in public ones, attended by foreigners present in Moscow, vigorous speeches from the floor, met with threats by the platform, were heartily supported and applauded by most of those present. When appeals were made for "democracy", the reaction was the shouting in unison of "FROM BELOW! FROM BELOW!"

One official comment was: "amongst the students of the junior courses, there is much childish mischief and desire to turn the University into a kind of discussion club where one can come and talk about socialist realism today, about democratic centralism tomorrow, etc." (*Bulletin of the Moscow University*, No. 2, 1957).

Earlier *Pravda* (November 25, 1956) had reported the presence of "disorganizers and lazy persons" among the student body of the Moscow "Bauman" Technological Institute, Malenkov's alma mater. The situation there had gone so far that "under the influence of a few bawlers", a group of students had even "tried to vote" on "whether it was worth carrying out the curriculum" laid down by the authorities—probably a reference to the compulsory lectures on Marxism-Leninism. Moscow art students from the Musical Conservatoire and the "Surikov" Art Institute— "and others"—came under fire in an article *Sovietskaya Kultura* (December 22, 1956), which also pointed to the "unhealthy moods" among Leningrad art students.

On December 27, 1956, *Pravda* published a version of a conference of the Moscow City Party Committee attended by the Soviet Minister of Higher Education, V. P. Elyutin, and summoned to discuss how to meet the student situation. "Individual students," said the report, "subjected to unhealthy moods, occasionally submit to the influence of alien ideology." The Party and Komsomol organizations were blamed "for their recent failure to provide leadership in the University". Later the Komsomol leaders were again blamed—this time by a representative of the Moscow Energetics Institute—for being "unable to give a wise and worthy rebuff to babblers and demagogues, who push their way forward here and there with their speeches" (*Komsomolskaya Pravda*, January 10, 1957).

Following sharp criticism on December 4, 1956, of the Leningrad "Lensoviet" Technological Institute and its "ultra-revolutionary" student "demagogues", *Komsomolskaya Pravda* accused students of the Leningrad Obrastsov Railway Transport Institute of having "unhealthy ideas and mistaken views" and of making "nihilistic" criticisms of "socialist realism" in the manuscript magazine, *Fresh Voices*.

The paper referred to all this as a "solitary instance", yet two weeks later it reported similar moods in the Zhdanov Leningrad University and the production of the manuscript magazine *Heresy* in the Leningrad Krupskaya Bibliotechnical Institute. On December 22, the organ of the Ministry of Culture, *Sovietskaya Kultura*, reported the presence of "unhealthy moods" among the 98,000 student members of the Cultural Workers Trade Union, including students of the Leningrad Repin Art Institute. The local *Leningradskaya Pravda* (December 11, 1956) reported passive resistance to Communist organized functions—for example, the World Youth Festival, then due to be held in Moscow. The Komosomol authors of the article claimed they had "many means and methods of struggle against such anti-public manifestations in the student milieu".

Another unexpected sector of Soviet student life where "harmful ideas" were reported was the armed forces. On December 19, 1956, *Sovietskii Flot* drew attention to the "harmful ideas" among naval students and "cases of idle talk in the appraisal of various phenomena and a reduction in the struggle against bourgeois . . . ideology penetrating our country from abroad".

At the time of the student riots in Tbilisi, Georgia, in March, 1956, almost all the 5,000 students of the Stalin University there were members of the Komsomol or of the Party itself. "It would appear," said the Georgian Communist newspaper, *Zarya Vostoka* (March 29, 1956), "that the influence of the Party and Komsomol organizations must be exceptionally great". The paper added: "In actual fact, this is not so." In August a special plenary session of the local Central Committee spoke of a "serious collapse in ideological work, especially among the youth".

The familiar phrase "unhealthy moods" was duly applied to Moldavian students in the leading article of December 20,

1956, issue of *Sovietskaya Moldavia*. In Byelorussia were found "Shameless elements, and all kinds of bawlers who express unfounded dissatisfaction with lectures and seminary studies and who introduce disorganization into the student milieu" (*Kommunist Byelorussii* No. 10, October, 1956). At Kharkov too, *Komsomolskaya Pravda* states, "one comes across demagogues, babblers and yellers who try to make capital out of some difficulty or another . . . and who hide behind pseudo-revolutionary phrases".

In Murmansk, "account must be taken of the fact that the Murmansk Province is a frontier area, and many young sailors go abroad. It was noted that individual representatives of youth, especially students, are rising to the bait of hostile propaganda and are expressing unwholesome views on our reality" (*Molodoi Kommunist*, No. 5, 1957).

Reports of student unrest come also from the former Baltic States. The fullest reactions to these were published in *Sovietskaya Litva* on December 9, 1956, reporting a speech by Snechkus, the Lithuanian Party Secretary. He spoke of "people alien to the Soviet student body" and of those "who had succumbed to lies disseminated by the class enemy". In Lithuania, indeed, there was a general outburst, in which students played the leading part with street demonstrations: "The armed rising of the reaction against the democratic régime in Hungary has encouraged the reactionaries in our republic as well. The remnants of the former anti-popular parties, the exploiting classes, the bourgeois-nationalist elements and their various helpmates, started to raise their head. Some of them covered themselves up by criticism, others by the mask of alleged democracy, but others tried completely openly to slander and to sow distrust in the policy of the Communist Party and the Soviet Government in Lithuania" (*Sovietskaya Litva*, December 9, 1956).

In Latvia too there were complaints of "alien influences

penetrating the student body", of "bourgeois propaganda" and of "incidents of amoral behaviour, dissoluteness and apolitical spirit among the youth" (*Soviet Latvia*, January 24, 1957). In Armenia there had been "crude political mistakes" and "rotten liberalism" (*Kommunist*, January 24, 1957). In Kazakhstan as well: "In the Kazakh State University individual students have begun to spread unhealthy ideas" (*Kommunist Kazakhstana*, February, 1957). And so on all over the USSR.

These manifestations were not only attacked. They were suppressed. A number of students seem to have been jailed, and more expelled—some of them for pro-Yugoslav "propaganda". In September, 1959 the Moscow papers revealed that certain students who had become actively "anti-Soviet" in 1956 had in the meantime been successfully "re-educated", by the police.

The "reform" of the Soviet educational system undertaken in 1955, which greatly reduces the number of full-time students, seems to have been at least partly motivated by a desire to discipline the unorthodox minds. In an address to the Komsomol (November 8, 1956) Khrushchev said: "It is essential to raise our vigilance, to devote greater attention to the correct upbringing of youth. . . . In improving educative work among youth, it is necessary to correct mistaken views and to give a rebuff to unhealthy phenomena." He accompanied this exhortation with a threat: "The system of admission to Higher Educational Establishments should be improved; it is necessary that only the best enter Higher Educational Establishments, and that they should be devoted to the cause of Lenin." He added: "If you do not like our order, which was won by our blood and by our work, then please go and work yourself, and others will come to study in your place."

In December, 1956, the Soviet Minister of Higher Education

demanded abolition of the principle of education for all according to ability. Leningrad Komsomol members were told that the "recommendation of a social organization, a factory or construction site will carry not less but more weight than the gold medal of the schoolboy of yesterday" (*Komsomolskaya Pravda*, December 28, 1956).

It should, incidentally, be pointed out that Khrushchev's claim about higher education, that enrolment at Soviet institutions was "four times greater than in Britain, France, West Germany and Italy combined", made at the 21st Party Congress in January, 1959, is quite unjustified. If we take full-time university students alone the British figure by itself is only just under the Soviet one (97,000 for 1957 as compared with 116,000 for 1956 respectively). For all university students, including part-time and correspondence, it is 107,000 compared to 166,000. It is difficult to obtain comparable figures for all "Higher Education" students as the ones assembled on both sides often include "further education" students who are perhaps doing only a few hours a week. On the other hand, British figures exclude commercial and professional colleges, courses for State nurses, and so on. Not allowing for this, the best available figures—covering all forms of Higher Education officially listed by either country —are: British, 2,346,000; Russian, 5,917,000. That is to say that the USSR, with four times the British population, has about $2\frac{1}{2}$ times the number of students. Although the various considerations mentioned above affect the true comparability of these figures, yet they make it clear enough that Khrushchev's claim can be maintained only by defining higher education in the Soviet Union very loosely and in Britain very strictly. On the other hand it is certainly true that a bigger effort than ours is being put into Soviet technical and scientific education. The question of how far results can be obtained in this field simply by increasing numbers and work is being debated by educationists here: but presumably the effect will not be negligible.

But regardless of figures, quality is important. If Khrushchev really intends, with the new proposals which make University education part-time except for certain special grades, to keep out the independent minds and to prevent orthodox ones from developing further, he is reducing the effectiveness of Soviet education.

It may be doubted, in any case, if such restraints will work any more. It is perfectly clear from the experiences of 1956 that underneath the rigours of official doctrine there is a deep desire for free discussion, and a deep thirst for new ideas. It would hardly be going too far to say that the huge apparatus of indoctrination has not succeeded.

No omen could be happier.

We are sometimes told of the enthusiasm of the Soviet's young people for the projects of the régime, such as the virgin lands in Kazakhstan. A picture in which all young people were systematically hostile to the established order would obviously be a false one. So would one in which enthusiasm reigns on every young face in the street, as much as it does in the posters on its walls. If the United Kingdom were ruled by a one-party Conservative régime and visitors relied largely on official handouts and visits to Primrose League Camps, they might well form a false impression.

There is a theory that the Soviet State can engage enthusiasm in a way in which democracies cannot. It certainly seems true that a section of the young people of any country can be possessed, or seem to be possessed, by State-sponsored enthusiasms in the absence of any others, as was seen with many of the younger generation in Germany in the 'thirties. There are certainly thousands upon thousands of young Soviet enthusiasts following the lead of the Komsomol Secretaries referred to in Chapter XI. But it is clear that in present circumstances they are not typical. When official organs attack a student for trying to secure cheap popularity by criticizing the régime, it is giving something away—that such criticism is the way to popularity with the young. And the young, after all, are the key to the future.

CHAPTER XIII

PROSPECTS

THE POSSIBILITIES OF future relations between ourselves and the Soviet Union include a true *détente*, in which
ideas, travellers and influences are freely exchanged and
exclusive claims to rectitude, on both sides, abandoned. They
include a permanent state of vigilance—of siege and counter-
siege. And it cannot be blinked that they include a third and
worse possibility—nuclear war.

Soviet military doctrine holds that in a future world war the
initial exchange of nuclear weapons would cause enormous
destruction, but the issue would then be decided in long-
drawn-out conventional campaigns. Meanwhile, we may
consider what there is on the Soviet side which makes such a
prospect even conceivable:—

the internal organization of the Soviet Union is one
which generates high tensions, likely to spread into the
international field. The USSR has built up a siege economy
where a huge and powerful war production and capital-
goods production is supported by inadequate consumer goods
production and a rickety agriculture;

the ideological monopoly in the Soviet Union is based on
the inculcation (which, as we have seen, has by no means
wholly succeeded) of the infallibility of a particular theory,
and of the necessity for permanent strife against believers in
other systems. This is an obviously unnatural and dangerous
situation;

The political structure of the USSR is one by which in the
past a dictator was able to enforce his will on the whole

country, in imposing a much resented economy organized against the natural tendencies of the population, and a single and embittered ideology contrary to the normal feelings of most Russians. The apparatus he built for doing this involves a vast and mendacious propaganda machinery—mendacious beyond the ordinary habit of politicians—and at the same time the maintenance of total secrecy on a wide range of matters, and a large and on occasion brutal secret police.

The present rulers have eliminated some of the worst excesses and reduced some others, but they employ much the same machinery of propaganda and repression, the same ideology, and much the same economic organization. Until there is a reasonable relaxation in these we cannot consider the USSR as being in any way devoted to peace, except a peace on their own terms—which is not of course to say that she wants or plans war. A truly peaceful Russia is one that will be based on a reasonable attitude to its own people, with some freedom of workers' and peasants' organisations, and with the state not in a position to suppress information and views, nor to decide everything without reference to the people.

The old machine was built by Stalin for Stalin's use. The corollary was that it needed a Stalin to use it. Stalin's successors are not men of his calibre—indeed it was a condition of his own survival that all men of anything like his capacity had been executed. Yet the enormous pressures produced by the system needed either that single-minded counter-pressure, or the letting off of some of the steam. The present rulers are not so firmly in the saddle as Stalin was, and disputes between them have already led to something like attempts by one faction to obtain support from social or political groups outside the central circle. Ideologies change under the pressure of events, and it is by no means impossible that the Soviet Union may evolve into a state which, formally democratic or not, is economically stable and more or less answers the desires of its population. Such a state would have no incentive to expansionism, and we could all live in harmony with it.

The present rulers, as far as they can, combat the idea that such an evolution is possible. "Revisionism" is now the major heresy: and that very fact shows how widespread it must be. An authoritative analysis of it was given in 1957 in the journal *In Aid of Political Self-Education* by Ponomarev, long one of Khrushchev's leading ideological assistants. Ponomarev lists seven ways in which the revisionists have gone wrong. They are not sufficiently sold on the theory that "imperialism" is preparing a new war. They deny the leading role of the Party. They think a peaceful transition to socialism possible and desirable. They are not sufficiently hostile to the Socialist parties. They do not appreciate "the advantages of socialism over bourgeois democracy". They are against "democratic centralism" inside the Party, and demand freedom to "criticize decisions which have been adopted". And they slip into the positions of "national communism" and "deny the significance of the experience of the Communist Party of the Soviet Union".

It will be seen that these deviations boil down to two central points. The first is the urging of a more flexible approach to the outer world and to non-Communists, and denial of the absolutely overriding nature of the opposition between Communism and everything else. The second is a repudiation of the right of the Party leaders to rule without question, and of the Russian Party leaders to rule other parties. On the first point, the revisionists point out that Soviet leaders *talk* in terms of a *détente* and of the possibility of a peaceful transition to socialism. And they ask them to follow the logical conclusions of their words. To some extent, in fact, the revisionists seem to be putting forward the worst of all heresies—look at the facts first, your prejudices second. But the questions of Party democracy and of Soviet leadership are the true centre of the struggle. The revisionists want, in Communist conditions, freedom of speech, a democratically organized Party and national independence.

The weak point in official theory has been found. And that is, the divergence between the Party's words and its deeds. The leaders are now faced with a situation in which many of their articulate followers have said in effect: "The Party programme speaks of inner party democracy. The Soviet Constitution guarantees freedom of speech. We ask for no more than you are already committed to giving us." This is extremely difficult to answer, since the leaders can scarcely admit (perhaps even to themselves) that they are not behaving in accordance with their expressed promises. Stalin, indeed, had a satisfactory answer—the firing squad and the labour camp. The present leadership is not, for various reasons, able easily to revert to 100 per cent terrorism, and even 90 per cent would not be enough. The alternative is compromise. No one can say whether Khrushchev and his associates might not, in the long run and in spite of all difficulties, prefer a reversion to full-scale terrorism. Such, of course, was the answer of the autocracies to the 1848 revolutions which temporary concessions, like those of 1956, had brought to a head. But the restored tyrannies never looked the same. The anathematized ideas could not be destroyed. And the despotism finally died by them.

For a generation the official line has made the question of the economic organization of society basic to all political argument. And the result has been, not only that every political freedom was sacrificed in the name of economic and social advance, but that the economic measures themselves got out of hand and led, as in Hungary and Poland, to crises far worse than those afflicting the capitalist system. At the

173

same time they led to the creation of an economically privi-leged stratum, so that even the egalitarian justification was not present. All this has now become obvious to everyone in the Soviet world who permits himself, or is permitted, to think at all. The area of disagreement has again been broadened to take in all spheres. When Khrushchev argues that Russian elections are freer than any others because under capitalism the worker only has a right to starve, his point is seen at once to be not merely false as to fact, but irrelevant even if true.

The Stalinist epoch was one of thoroughgoing despotism. The movement of ideas, and the necessities of the present situation, seem to indicate that the Soviet future must be an evolution into far greater freedoms. But when has a half-way house between freedom and despotism ever flourished as more than a temporary makeshift?

The new social forces in Russia which make the Krushchev régime look so old-fashioned have a great deal in common with the democratic moods of the last century. What the "revisionists", the writers and the students and all the others are asking for consciously, and the social offenders less consciously, is basically just freedom of speech and a share in determining policy.

To see the Khrushchev epoch in perspective is a little difficult for us. The man actually in power in a major state always looms big at the time. But it is often true that after-wards he is seen as a fairly minor, transitional figure, beset by forces outside his control, and practically forgotten in a generation. In the 1780s Turgot or Necker might have been thought of as giants dominating the greatest state in Europe, and operating "liberal" policies which would save the autocracy.

Khrushchev's economic reorganization, agricultural crash programme and other adventurous moves are yet kept

174

within strict limits and are subject to hasty reversals. They are the actions of a man who knows that the old system does not work, yet is quite unwilling to make any substantial change. This is usual behaviour on the part of a transitional ruler. And, as so often, the actions serve to loosen up the structure of the autocracy, even though that was not their real intention.

The Soviet Union is ruled by party officials who have certain fixed ideas about the nature of the desirable organization of society. Changes will not some about without considerable resistance from them. But one thing seems certain: the régime will either evolve peacefully or it will perish.

For thinking people even in Russia have understood that ideological formulae are not an adequate substitute for examination of the facts; that a régime is best judged by its acts rather than its slogans; and, above all, that those who rise to the top under the present Communist system are not likely to be the best judges of realities, let alone ideas, in spite of their skill at manipulating the political machine. This new understanding on the part of Russians of good will and good sense is bound in the long run to be fatal to any who may attempt to go against "the iron laws of history" with which they have so often threatened others.

For Soviet society is beset, as we have seen, by stresses which must lead to change. A Russia at peace with itself, and able to pour out to the world the vast riches of its life and culture and to receive freely in return, would be one of the finest components of a world community. It is a clear and genuine possibility, and one which can give us heart and encouragement as we face, and do everything in our power to avert, the other, more terrible possibilities of our time.